P9-DUI-889

Getting Started with Demand-Driven Acquisitions for E-Books

ALA TechSource purchases fund advocacy, awareness, and accreditation programs for library professionals worldwide.

Getting Started with Demand-Driven Acquisitions for E-Books

A LITA Guide

Theresa S. Arndt

ALA TechSource

An imprint of the American Library Association

CHICAGO   2015

THERESA S. ARNDT is the associate director for library resources and administration at the Waidner-Spahr Library at Dickinson College in Carlisle, Pennsylvania. Her responsibilities include coordinating all aspects of collections management and e-resources services. She has worked at multiple libraries over her twenty-year career, managing various library services including reference, information literacy, and outreach. She earned her bachelor's degree from Case Western Reserve University, and her master's degree in library science from SUNY Buffalo. She can be reached at arndtt@dickinson.edu.

© 2015 by Theresa S. Arndt

Extensive effort has gone into ensuring the reliability of the information in this book; however, the publisher makes no warranty, express or implied, with respect to the material contained herein.

ISBNs
978-0-8389-1314-7 (paper)
978-0-8389-1322-2 (PDF)
978-0-8389-1323-9 (ePub)
978-0-8389-1324-6 (Kindle)

Library of Congress Cataloging-in-Publication Data

Arndt, Theresa S.
    Getting started with demand-driven acquisitions for e-books : a LITA guide / Theresa S. Arndt.
        pages   cm
    Includes bibliographical references and index.
    ISBN 978-0-8389-1314-7 (print : alk. paper) — ISBN 978-0-8389-1323-9 (epub) — ISBN 978-0-8389-1322-2 (pdf) — ISBN 978-0-8389-1324-6 (kindle)
    1. Libraries—Special collections—Electronic books. 2. Patron-driven acquisitions (Libraries) 3. Electronic books. 4. Libraries and electronic publishing. I. Title.
    Z692.E4A76 2015
    025.2'84—dc23   2014046392

Cover image ©scyther5/Shutterstock, Inc. Text composition in the Berkeley and Avenir typefaces.

This paper meets the requirements of ANSI/NISO Z39.48–1992 (Permanence of Paper).

⊗ Printed in the United States of America

19 18 17 16 15   5 4 3 2 1

To my husband and my best friend, Donald,
for the many years of constant
and ongoing love and support
he has given to me
through all my endeavors.

Contents

Acknowledgments

Thanks to Kirk Doran, who was instrumental in helping to create the original internal DDA checklist from which sprouted the concept for this guide. In addition to authoring the chapter on cataloging, Kirk also reviewed the final manuscript. Thanks also to Jessica L. Howard, a colleague who generously made time in her busy schedule to review and give comments on the final manuscript. Both Kirk's and Jess's notes helped to improve the final product greatly, but any errors and deficiencies are solely my responsibility. Thanks also to the entire staff of the Waidner-Spahr Library for always asking good questions, proposing good ideas, and generally making all the work we do better and more fun

Introduction

When our library decided to investigate demand-driven acquisitions (DDA) for e-books in 2012 we started, as all good librarians do, by reviewing the professional literature as well as other sources. We found a few published case studies, and we also attended several conference presentations and webinar presentations. We had extensive conversations with various vendors. We combed the publications on e-books available at that time, which had some mentions of DDA. We found a body of literature on DDA as it had been used for print books which did provide information on the overall concept. The literature on e-book DDA was still emerging, and was less helpful in addressing the practical steps required to implement DDA exclusively with e-books. The problem was we didn't know what we might be forgetting to ask, because we didn't know what we didn't know! We also realized that decisions we made along the way might have unintended consequences later, but we weren't sure what those might be. What we really wanted was a list of all the many questions we should be asking ourselves and vendors, issues we should be considering, decisions we would need to make along the way. Such a list would be even better if it explained the implications of each choice. We also wanted some detailed, practical "how to" advice on how to get our DDA program up and running. In the end, we began creating our own "checklist" of questions that grew larger and longer the more we realized how much there was to consider and how many decisions we needed to make. This guide grew out of a desire to share this list of questions, decision points, and practical knowledge with other librarians who are interested in getting started with e-book DDA, and to help them think through the many choices that need to be made.

DDA has worked well for our library, increasing instant access to more e-books for our users, while holding down overall library book purchasing cost increases. We know that the DDA titles we end up paying for are all actually used, unlike the print and e-books that we buy based on profiling, alerts, reviews, librarian-selector judgment, and user recommendations alone. It has become an integral part of our overall collections strategy, although that strategy continues to include firm orders in print and e-book format for titles we consider "core" to our collection. This guide assumes a positive attitude toward DDA implementation, but potential problems are also pointed out. Although examples from the literature and from our small academic library's experience are given for illustrative purposes, this guide is primarily intended to help you plan an e-book DDA program that is right for your library, by prompting you with questions which will help you make decisions. In this way, we hope to help other libraries shape DDA programs that are suited to local circumstances. Library missions and the population of library users they serve are variable, so the implementation will need to be customized. While much of the research literature on DDA comes from academic libraries, all library types are using DDA, and the questions posed in this guide will be relevant across library types, although the decisions and choices made by those libraries may differ.

As you work through the questions, remember that you probably will not be able to get everything you would ideally want in terms of e-book features, license terms, and pricing models, but some things will be negotiable. The e-book market and DDA models continue to evolve as publishers seek to meet the needs of the library market, while protecting their own need to make a profit. Ask for what you want, but be prepared to negotiate with flexibility by prioritizing your goals for your DDA program. There will also be various trade-offs in terms of staff time and direct dollar costs. This guide is intended to be practical. At times we will suggest that you consider doing nothing. Care and feeding of an e-book DDA program can eat up endless amounts of time if you let it, but some of the time spent may not be worth the small benefit gained.

Although it is divided into separate chapters, it is highly recommended that you read through the entire guide. There is overlap between chapters, but DDA programs are made up of a lot of different moving parts that are interrelated and discussed throughout the guide. For example, policy decisions will influence your ability to budget for DDA, and your choices of vendors will influence your workflow decisions. Unless you are running a one-person library, you will probably want to take a team approach to implementing DDA from the start. At our relatively small library, two librarians, including a cataloger, as well as an acquisitions para-professional were involved in thinking through the various DDA setup decisions. It is our hope that this guide will help you go into DDA with more confidence and will help you avoid surprises.

What this guide does not do is provide a comprehensive overview of all e-book management issues libraries face, although these are touched on as they relate specifically to DDA. This guide assumes you already have some familiarity with providing purchased or subscribed e-books to your users, or will seek out the many excellent books on general e-book management to gain that knowledge (Kaplan 2012, Polanka 2012, Roncevic 2013).

Despite early concerns about e-book DDA, many libraries are now routinely and successfully using it. The National Information Standards Organization (NISO) DDA Working Group conducted a survey in August 2013 which garnered responses from 81 mostly academic libraries that used DDA, 56 for e-books only, and 23 more for e-books and print. The majority reported that their programs were effective and met the goals their library had set (NISO DDA Working Group 2013).

Most of the downsides of DDA that are raised are actually concerns about e-books in general, such as the timely availability of new titles in e-book format, the differential in cost between print and e-book versions of titles, digital rights management restrictions, simultaneous use concerns, turnaways due to simultaneous use limits, long term preservation and access concerns, complaints about usability of e-book platform interfaces, accessibility for people with disabilities, and interlibrary loan restrictions. These are issues of concern with all library e-book acquisitions, and are important, but they are not specific to a DDA method. Other concerns relate to user behavior, such as a situation in which only one individual uses a single title many times, or one person is the only user of many titles. This sort of activity also occurs with any library collection, and is not specific to DDA. Every library has "frequent flyers" as well as potential users who, alas, never use anything from the library collection. At our library we would be delighted if every firm order title we purchased actually got used at least once by even one person, and we are also delighted to see a single user check out multiple books.

Throughout this guide variations in DDA programs are discussed, as the options offered by vendors are evolving in response to the library market. DDA for e-books is still an emerging service. The NISO DDA Working Group consisting of publishers, vendors, and librarians issued "recommended practices" for DDA in June 2014 (NISO DDA Working Group). These are not binding, but will help serve as guidelines for libraries and vendors to find mutually agreeable and sustainable models for DDA in the future.

As with any rapidly evolving model, there are some variations in the vocabulary used for DDA. For consistency throughout this guide, one term has been chosen for each concept, and a glossary is included at the end of the guide with reference to some of the common synonyms that you may encounter.

What Is Demand-Driven Acquisition, and Why Do It?

D emand-driven acquisitions (DDA) is a system for facilitating discovery of a title that the library does not currently own and, upon request, quickly buying it for the library collection and providing access to the user. Most often the term refers to monograph acquisitions, and it is alternatively referred to in the library literature as "patron-driven acquisitions" (PDA), "patron-initiated purchase of e-books" (PIPE), or "patron (or demand) -driven collection development." Throughout this guide the abbreviation DDA will be used. Although DDA has been used by libraries for many years to acquire print books, the focus of this guide is exclusively on e-books, because that technology allows delivery that is truly "on demand" for the user. Many libraries use a "short-term loan" option prior to a DDA purchase, which will be referred to in this guide by the abbreviation STL.

In a sense, librarians have always practiced a form of DDA. Whether it was buying materials specifically recommended by users, titles that were widely and positively reviewed and thus likely to be requested, or books receiving a demand bump from celebrity endorsement, libraries have always reacted to the market force of user demand. As Barbara Quint recently put it, "Buying stuff somebody wants, instead of just what a vendor has plenty of . . . what a concept!" (Quint 2014).

There are many potential advantages of e-book DDA. Users can be provided with access to a much wider array of materials than the library could afford to purchase on a speculative basis, and their choices are not limited to books for which a librarian was able to predict interest. Because the e-book specifically chosen by the user can be delivered instantly, without waiting for an ordering process or interlibrary loan delivery, there is increased library responsiveness to actual user needs. Traditional methods of collection development are often based on subject divisions, which may ignore emerging genres or interdisciplinary subjects that are of interest to users, but are unknown to librarians. Peripheral titles can be offered without risk that funds are wasted if they are not used. DDA can also be a more efficient way of providing access to a large variety of titles, by using a profile rather than labor-intensive title-by-title selection or selector approval of purchases. For subjects about which there are many published titles, but low predictability about which specific titles will be used, DDA can be a good solution. Even on a small scale, DDA can serve as a valuable supplement to other collection development activities.

YBP Library Service Inc.'s 2014 Annual Book Price Update on the titles their company profiles indicates that the majority of large publishers published more books than in the prior year, and the list price of books increased an average of 3.5 percent per year in the last ten years (YBP Library Services, 2014, www.ybp.com/book_price_update.html). It is becoming increasingly difficult for any library to keep up with such publishing trends through traditional acquisitions approaches. DDA provides the potential for budget savings by ensuring the purchase of only materials that are actually used at least once, and reducing the purchase of materials that are not used—a true "just in time" rather than "just in case" acquisitions approach. Since DDA typically provides some sort of limited "free" browsing time, users have the opportunity to evaluate the usefulness of a title, prior to the library spending money to acquire it. See figure 1.1 for a comparison of a traditional versus a DDA acquisitions workflow.

Underlying the DDA premise is also the assumption that books used by one, or a few, users are more likely to be used in the future by other users of the library, making it logical to purchase the books rather than just borrow them through interlibrary loan. Multiple studies by academic libraries using DDA indicate that materials acquired in this way are as likely or even more likely to be used in the future. The way to think about DDA is not as an additional cost burden, but as a way to spend your budget on things that are actually used. How much money is your library spending on books that are never used, even after many years in the collection? DDA seeks to prevent this money from being wasted. As a result of not buying unused books, some libraries find that DDA actually saves money on their overall book budgets, especially when implemented with an STL component that avoids paying full list price for a book used only a few times. The money saved through avoiding such expenditures can be reallocated to other acquisitions or library needs.

Traditional E-Book Acquisitions Workflow	DDA E-Book Acquisitions Workflow
An approval plan profile (if used) is established with library service provider, other vendors. Alerts, vendor catalogs, and book reviews are consulted to select titles for purchase. Selection of individual titles is made by library staff. Titles recommended by users are considered for purchase.	A DDA profile is established with vendor(s), using subject and non-subject parameters, including a price cap.
As individual orders are placed, an order record is created in the integrated library system.	
Titles are received.	
Records for newly owned items are added to the catalog.	Discovery records for all profiled titles are added to the catalog.
Additional access points are established (e.g., in the library discovery layer).	Additional access points are established (e.g., in the library discovery layer).
Invoices are received and paid prior to any use.	
Title may or may not ever be used.	
	"Selection" by the end user occurs at point of need. Purchase is triggered only when the title is actually used; an invoice is received and paid following use.
	A point-of-invoice record is overlaid on the discovery record in the catalog. Included order data generates an order record in the integrated library system acquisitions module.
Titles remain available for possible future use, having already been paid for.	Titles that are triggered and purchased remain available for possible future use once paid for.
	Unused discovery records may remain available, with no payment required if no trigger ever occurs. Vendor(s) may remove titles from DDA availability. If funds for DDA are exhausted, DDA discovery records will be suppressed or removed from the catalog by the library.

FIGURE 1.1

Comparison of traditional vs. DDA acquisitions workflow

While setting up a DDA system will initially require a great deal of thought and time, it may provide savings of time in some areas of staffing. Depending on the exact approach and workflows you adopt, it can reduce time needed for title-by-title selection or acquisitions decisions, physical book processing, and invoice processing. This staff time can be reallocated for other activities and service offerings. However, DDA may require more staff time for setting up profiles with vendors and for ongoing catalog record maintenance.

- ☐ **What is your library's mission?**
- ☐ **What is your collection philosophy?**
- ☐ **What are the relative values you place on access vs. ownership?**

The extent to which you rely on DDA is the extent to which you are willing to put the building of the library collection in the hands of your users. Collection philosophies of libraries run along a spectrum. If your library places more emphasis on access, you may take a more utilitarian approach to acquisitions, seeking to acquire primarily books that will be used in the near term by the users of your library. Ideally you will see a high percentage of materials actively being used in the very near future. Your library may place a higher reliance on subscription collections, lease plans such as McNaughton, and interlibrary loan. A DDA system that includes STL fits in well with this approach.

If your library's mission and philosophy place more of an emphasis on long-term local ownership of collections, you may seek to acquire materials that are considered important for the collection without concern for whether they will be used in the near future. This philosophy is that someone, someday may want the item, perhaps after the current librarians are long gone, and it presumes that traditional models of selection and collection are good at predicting what those future important works will be, since no library can buy everything. Within budget limits, this requires a tightly focused collection policy and clear criteria for what will and will not be purchased. DDA need not replace proactive acquisition approaches to collection development. It may be used as a supplement to traditional collection building, to acquire works that librarian selectors might miss, as well as to provide faster access to materials for users' immediate needs.

Many libraries today take a pragmatic approach to collection building, seeking to acquire, in advance of user requests, a core collection of books that are expected to serve both short- and long-term user needs. Given the impossibility of predicting all user needs and interests, as well as a limited budget, the local collection is of necessity supplemented with interlibrary loan service. DDA with or without STL can provide an additional, effective tool for fast service to users and supplemental collection building.

- ☐ To what extent are your current means of collection development fulfilling or not fulfilling your collection goals?
- ☐ Are your current means of collection development adequately meeting all user needs in a timely fashion?
- ☐ What percentage of published books, that are relevant to your mission, can your library actually purchase now?
- ☐ Do you have librarians with both the time and expert knowledge to purchase in every area your users may be interested in?
- ☐ Are all librarians able to devote sufficient time to collection responsibilities across all their areas of subject responsibility?
- ☐ Might interdisciplinary subject areas or emerging genres be neglected by your current collection methods?

5

There are discussions in the literature that articulate concerns about DDA's potentially negative impact on library collections. One concern is that DDA will lead to an idiosyncratic collection. But most libraries already include some responsiveness to user requests or recommendations in their collection building methods, and even librarians are subject to individual preferences, biases, and limitations of knowledge. A study of five libraries found that DDA resulted in collecting that was much like that done by librarians. The DDA selections were "no more narrow, skewed, or individually focused" than those made by librarians selecting in a traditional manner (Price and McDonald 2009). Concerns about using STL within a DDA program are that these "selections" do not build the collection, but this is also what happens with interlibrary loan, only without instantaneous delivery. Presumably, if you are reading this guide, you have already decided that some level of DDA is appropriate for your library, and it is not the purpose of this guide to talk you out of it! However, thinking through potential concerns may help you both confirm your decision, and prepare to articulate your reasons for those in your administrative hierarchy and user base who may have questions or concerns.

☐ What do you hope to achieve by implementing demand-driven acquisitions?

☐ How important are each of the potential benefits to your library? What are your priorities?

☐ Do you want to maximize access to a wide array of information at the lowest possible cost, with less concern about adding to your permanent collection?

☐ Do you want to emphasize purchase of titles that are actually used, to build your permanent collection?

☐ Are you trying to save money, by reducing money spent on unused or lightly used books?

☐ Are you trying to maintain your current spending, but perhaps spend it more usefully?

While there are multiple benefits possible, it is helpful to identify your library's priorities for DDA. Your answer to these questions will influence the specific ways in which you implement and assess DDA at your library. Potential benefits include improved user service through fast delivery of a wider array of titles, cost savings or better use of funds by avoiding the purchase of titles that are never used, and reduction in staff time for selection and acquisitions activities. However, note that staff time needed for other, new activities will likely increase. More details about how to shape your DDA program to meet specific goals are provided in the chapters of this guide on access, budgeting, and administration.

☐ What will be the place of DDA in your overall collection strategy?

☐ How will DDA be used to compliment other collection-building techniques, such as approval plans?

Keeping in mind that not all titles are available as e-books, and not all e-books are made available for DDA by publishers, decide what role DDA will fill in your overall approach to building your collection.

An aggressive approach would be to have as many titles as possible available only through DDA. In other words, your library would cease buying any books just-in-case, and only buy a book when a user actually wanted to use it. This would eliminate the purchase of any book that would never be used. It is a radical rethinking of the traditional approach to building and maintaining a local library "collection." It also may increase the unpredictability of budgeting, although you could just decide to cut off purchasing when funds were expended, turning to ILL for the remainder of the budget year, assuming you have budgeted enough funds for that service.

Some libraries serving large populations and consortial groups participating in DDA have found that the money they budgeted for DDA ran out before the end of their budget year, but this has not been the case even for all large DDA pilots. Careful setup of a DDA profile will minimize spending on titles "inappropriate" for your library's collection, and allowing STLs prior to purchase will lower costs by preventing purchase of e-books used only once or a few times.

A less radical approach is to combine DDA of e-books with affordable subscription e-book collections and "core" purchased e-books. This approach can serve to satisfy a user population that is a voracious consumer of e-books within the constraints of the library budget. Librarians familiar with the needs and reading habits of their local user population probably are able to predict some of the titles that will actually be used. Analysis of circulation and interlibrary loan patterns can help with these predictions. Other titles may be considered supplemental, of peripheral interest, or "nice to have" but not "need to have." These latter titles could be good candidates for DDA, knowing that the library will only end up paying for them if they are used.

7

___

- [ ] Do you know how and to what extent your current collection is actually being used?
- [ ] How many unique titles are you getting for your users via interlibrary loan?
- [ ] Do your interlibrary loan patterns suggest areas in which you have collection gaps?
- [ ] Should you have considered purchasing the titles borrowed through interlibrary loan, instead of the titles you did purchase, but that were never used?

Assuming that you purchase books on the expectation that they will be used, are you certain such use is actually taking place? Studies have long shown that library selectors are only marginally good at purchasing books that are later used. Multiple studies of academic libraries, including large research libraries and smaller libraries, have found that a high percentage of print books—typically 40–50 percent—do not circulate after as many as ten years in the stacks. Prior to implementing DDA, we examined circulation statistics at our library and found that 66 percent had not circulated a year after purchase. Since our primary mission is to support the current curriculum and our budget is far from unlimited, this represented a large percentage of our book budget not being used to support current needs and supported our decision to implement DDA. Of course the number of unused books will vary from library to library. Knowing the actual use of your current collection will be valuable in thinking about how DDA fits into your overall collection development strategy, and in assessing the success of your DDA program down the line. It is also useful should you need to make a case to stakeholders for why you are implementing a DDA program.

Local Policy Considerations and DDA Management

Implementing a DDA program involves a lot of decisions and choices. Although there are many common elements, there is also flexibility in adapting DDA to your local practices and aligning it with your existing policies. You will also need to think about staffing, and decide which aspects of DDA can be integrated into your existing workflows, and which will require rethinking your operations. Libraries with both large and small staffs are successfully implementing DDA programs. It is possible to create a workable program with greater or lesser degrees of complexity and customization. An increasing number of vendors are offering DDA options, making it easier for even small libraries to get support for establishing and maintaining a program. This chapter discusses various policy and management decisions that you will need to make.

☐ **Which library staff will be involved in the initial setup of your DDA program?**

Initial stages in implementing a DDA program involve deciding whether you will use a library services provider intermediary, gathering information on various vendors and deciding which to use (perhaps more than one), reviewing and negotiating contract terms, setting up the discovery pool profile, and making the various policy decisions outlined elsewhere in this guide. One approach to getting started is to have existing library staff responsible for closely related functions fulfill those same functions for DDA program setup. Alternatively, you may decide that one or

two point people should work on the DDA program setup, consulting and inform-
ing other library staff along the way. This is the approach we took in our library.
The collections manager and cataloger became our local DDA experts, developed
recommendations, and conducted the initial setup. In this way fewer people had
to wade through all the details during the information gathering and early implementation phases. Other librarians and staff were consulted as needed to approve
the overall plan, and weigh in on policy decisions. Since our library has only 25
staff, including 10 librarians, this approach made the best use of everyone's time.

- [ ] Which vendors offer the titles that you want to provide in
  e-book format with a DDA option?
- [ ] Will you work with a library services provider, with an e-book
  aggregator, or with individual publishers?
- [ ] If you want to use a library services provider (e.g., YBP, Ingram/
  Coutts) as a DDA intermediary, which e-book publishers and
  aggregators do they work with?

Not all books are available as e-books, and even if they are there may be a lag of
eight weeks or more between the release of a book in print and the e-book edition
if there ever is one. Within the subset of books available in e-book format, is a still
smaller subset of titles made available for DDA. Some publishers, though not all,
and various aggregators offer DDA for e-books. Most aggregators will advertise the
availability of tens of thousands of titles, but are they the tens of thousands of titles
of interest to your library's users? Ask to see a list of titles, or at least publishers,
to gauge the appropriateness for your library. Loading large numbers of irrelevant
DDA e-book records into your catalog can create a lot of clutter for your users to
wade through to get to titles that interest them, so ask what the profiling options
are for filtering content to that most appropriate for your users.

Decide if you wish to work with a single vendor, or with multiple vendors. Some
libraries choose to work with multiple vendors and run several complementary
DDA programs to expand the pool of titles available. However, working with multiple vendors will increase the likelihood of duplicate titles entering your discovery
pool(s), and requires keeping track of varying licensing terms and triggers. If you
are considering working with multiple vendors, think about the additional and
more complex administrative workload that will create for library staff. If you are
just getting started with DDA, consider starting with a single vendor or aggregator
to get familiar with the process and establish local workflows.

You can set up a DDA program with a library services provider (e.g., YBP, Ingram/Coutts), an e-book aggregator (e.g., ebrary, EBSCO, JSTOR, Library Ideas), or with an increasing number of individual publishers. There are pros and cons related to the type of vendor you choose to work with when implementing your DDA program. Also, no one vendor can give you access to all the potential DDA titles you might wish to provide to your users.

The main advantage of working directly with a publisher is that most publisher platforms do not impose digital rights management (DRM) restrictions on the content. Of course, working with only one publisher greatly restricts the title list available. Working with multiple individual publishers provides a broader range of titles, but also means your users will have to deal with multiple platforms. This may have a negative impact on service by confusing users, and also can make management and trouble-shooting difficult for library staff. Administration and monitoring of use statistics will also have to be done on multiple platforms. Keep in mind that some publishers still do not offer individual titles via DDA models. Indeed, some do not yet offer individual e-books for sale, but only sell their e-book content as part of packages.

Using an e-book aggregator provides access to a wide range of publishers on a single platform. Assuming the platform is decent, users and library staff can get used to a single system. No aggregator includes all publishers, but you may be able to find one that works with many or the majority of publishers you would want to access. For broad subject and genre coverage, consider an aggregator that has agreements with a wide range of publishers (some of the larger aggregators for the library market are ebrary/EBL, EBSCO, Overdrive, and MyiLibrary). Your library may already have a good working relationship with an aggregator for subscribed or purchased e-book content. Working with an aggregator also simplifies license negotiation, as the library signs a contract only with the aggregator, who negotiates standardized terms with a variety of publishers. An aggregator will provide you with tools for creating a profile of titles to include in your discovery pool, and for monitoring title use and spending. The downside of aggregators is the imposition of DRM restrictions that exceed those imposed on most individual publisher platforms, such as limits on printing and downloading.

Library service providers can add value with systems that provide for sophisticated profiling, customization of MARC records, integrated acquisitions workflows, and centralized invoicing. They work with multiple publishers and aggregators, thus allowing you to further centralize management of your DDA program while expanding the pool of titles available. Because they work with a large number of libraries and many types of libraries, library service providers have broad knowl-edge of various DDA options, and they can answer questions and offer guidance as you develop your DDA program. If you are already working with a library ser-vice provider, you will not need to establish a new vendor relationship for DDA. Because of your acquisitions staff's familiarity with the vendor's services, you should have an easier time incorporating DDA into your existing selection and acquisi-tions workflows. If the majority of your other acquisitions are through the same library service provider, de-duping your DDA discovery pool against your existing print and e-book holdings should also be easier. The downsides of working with a library service provider are that some publishers will not make DDA content available through third party vendors or may impose additional license or access restrictions on such content. You also remove yourself from negotiating terms and pricing directly with individual publishers, although some librarians will see that as an advantage. The library service provider perspective on DDA has been described in several helpful articles (Forzetting and Gallagher 2012; Harwell 2012). See appendix A for an example of how a DDA program works with a library services provider and an e-book aggregator.

- ☐ How will you select titles for the "DDA decision pool" and "DDA discovery pool"?
- ☐ What criteria will you use for including or excluding titles from your discovery pool? Who will be involved in making these decisions?
- ☐ Who will decide the parameters for the discovery pool profile?
- ☐ Will you implement DDA across your entire collection, or only with selected segments?

While it is possible to create a discovery pool through title-by-title selection, most libraries choose the profile method. Setting up a profile with the publisher, vendor, or your library services provider requires work up front, but is less labor-intensive once established. Consider criteria such as appropriateness to your collection (how-ever you define that), subject, cost, publishers to include or exclude, genre (e.g., fiction, nonfiction, reference works, cookbooks, textbooks), reading level (adult, young adult, juvenile, academic level), publication date (include new/current titles only, or also include retrospective titles, titles reissued in e-book format), language, country of publication, and pricing/licensing model.

It is important to spend adequate time setting up the profile that will create your DDA discovery pool. The profile will determine which titles are included or screened out, depending on how you look at it. Your vendor should provide a variety of administrative tools to customize the profile of your DDA discovery pool so that it includes only titles most in line with your collection guidelines. This is typically accomplished through use of standard library classification schemes (LC, Dewey), or via vendor-specific subject categorization schemes. Non-subject parameters can also typically be specified, such as year of publication, cost, publisher, genre, language, country of publication, and so on.

Some libraries have chosen to wade into DDA slowly by conducting pilots with only a few segments of the collection. This allows you to test out both workflows and user service on a smaller scale. And you might decide that DDA is an appropriate collection model for some purposes but not others. Rutgers, for example, chose to start with math and computer science, because they knew that the users of those subjects were already consistent users of e-books, and so the format would be acceptable to them. They also knew that over 40 percent of the books they were acquiring in these subjects through traditional strategies were not used after four years. A user satisfaction survey also showed that their computer science students wanted access to materials the library was not acquiring. Rather than using a profile, they chose a more discriminating approach, by selecting each title individually for inclusion in their DDA discovery pool. They did this so that librarian-selectors could ensure that each title included was appropriate for their collection goals. Implementing DDA on this small scale for a receptive audience primed the program for success (De Fino and Lo 2011).

Some libraries choose to have a different profile for DDA than for standard collection building. If you work with multiple vendors or publishers for DDA, you may choose to, or have to, set up a different profile with each. We chose to use our entire existing YBP profile, developed originally for print book acquisition, so there was no additional work required to identify the "DDA decision pool." This provided an expedient way to get started with DDA, which reflected decisions made by all the librarian-selectors in the past. Including all subject areas allowed us to see which subjects our users would actually use via DDA, without the librarians' making any assumptions. We added a few additional profile stipulations for DDA, the most significant of which was a price cap so that users could not trigger the purchase of extremely expensive works, such as specialized encyclopedias. These works still show up in our alert profile for librarians to consider, but we did not want a single user to be able to trigger a purchase of such titles.

In addition, any titles in the YBP Gobi system that are eligible for DDA may be selected manually, even if they are not in our selection profile. At the start, YBP estimated that 35 percent of our existing profiled titles would be available as DDA titles. This still broadens discovery potential considerably for our users, since we do not automatically purchase everything in our profile, but just use it as a screening tool from which we firm order selected print and e-books, subject to budgetary constraints.

- ☐ For your initial DDA discovery pool, what publication dates do you want to include?
- ☐ Do you want your initial discovery pool to include a retrospective list of titles? Or do you only want to provide DDA access to newly published e-books?
- ☐ What publication year range will you include in your ongoing DDA program?

The decisions you make here have implications for the number of DDA titles in your initial discovery pool. If you include only newly published e-books going forward, your DDA pool will initially be small and will grow gradually. If you decide to do a retrospective inclusion, you will start out with a much larger DDA pool. Consider working with your vendor to de-dupe the DDA title list against your current holdings. The larger the DDA pool, the more likely that users will encounter and trigger DDA loans and purchases, so consider the budgetary implications of your decision. For an initial pilot, you may wish to load only current DDA e-books, and consider a retrospective load later after you have had time to evaluate your library's experience with DDA.

One caveat regarding use of "publication date" as a criterion: the e-book release date may not align with the title's publication date. Older imprints released as e-books may carry the e-book version release date, and thus appear to be newer works than they actually are. This can make a title seem contemporary when it is really a sort of electronic "reprint," and it is important to be aware of this if you want to focus on acquiring new works, or avoid buying titles that may already be in your collection.

Discuss with your vendor how they are determining whether you are getting access to "frontlist" (contemporary) titles vs. "backlist" (older) titles for your initial discovery pool load. Also ask about profile settings that will help you include only the publication years that you want, as titles are added to your discovery pool in the future. We decided to only include titles in our DDA discovery pool that carried a current year publication date, but we could have chosen to include current plus one or more past years, or all publication years.

☐ **Will you mediate use (purchase) to avoid "inappropriate" acquisitions, cost overruns, or duplicate purchases?**

Some libraries chose to mediate purchases to avoid "inappropriate" acquisitions (purchase of titles that are not within the scope of the library's collections guidelines), to have more control over spending, or to avoid purchase of duplicate titles. Typically e-book DDA is unmediated, and the content available is controlled through subject profiling as well as non subject parameters (e.g., cost caps). Cost risk is further controlled through use of a set amount placed on deposit with the vendor or budgeted up front. It is possible to set up a fully mediated DDA, whereby a user can not directly trigger an STL or purchase of an e-book without library staff approval. One reason favoring mediation is to avoid duplicate purchase of e-books acquired through other means, such as through purchase of publisher packages or via standing orders. However, careful profiling should be explored as a preferred means of excluding duplicate titles from your discovery pool. Mediation will result in an additional cost in staff time and delay in user access. While mediated DDAs have been used for many years for print book acquisitions, most libraries doing e-book DDA use a carefully profiled, but unmediated access approach. A hybrid approach is to mediate only those requests that exceed preestablished thresholds for price, rather than to exclude records for more expensive titles from the discovery pool.

15

☐ What constitutes a "trigger" for the vendor(s) with which you will be working?

☐ How much and what kind of free browsing is allowed prior to a trigger?

☐ If using short-term loans, how long or for what actions does the title continue to be available on the first loan before a second short-term loan or a purchase is triggered?

☐ Does the user have to log off in a particular way to cease access that may count as time toward a trigger, or is there an automatic time-out prior to a trigger if use is not active?

A "trigger" is the action by a user that results in a cost to the library. Depending on how you have set up your program, it will generate either a short-term loan cost or a purchase cost. Be sure you understand what actions, over what length of time, constitute a trigger under your contract, as they vary with the vendor and publisher. Triggering events can include the number of clicks on the content of the e-book, which may or may not include the table of contents, index, as well as the main text; cutting and pasting a piece of text; printing one or more pages; downloading a portion of the book or the entire book; viewing a certain number of pages or a certain amount of text; or "continuous use" of a title for a certain amount of time. Imagine a situation in which a user clicks on an e-book link, looks at a few pages, and decides the title is not of interest. Or a user opens an e-book and then walks away from the computer, leaving it on the screen. Would such brief use result in a charge to the library? Some vendors are more generous than others, and for example, will allow a significant period of free browsing, or exclude viewing of tables of contents and indexing from counting toward triggering. A reasonable amount of free browsing addresses the common concern that users will trigger an STL or purchase for an e-book that they quickly determine is not really of interest after all. Of course, traditional acquisitions can result in inadvertent purchases of undesirable books as well, since libraries often make purchase decisions based only on predetermined subject profiles, brief bibliographic information, or publisher promotional materials.

- ☐ Will you incorporate a short-term loans (STL) option in your DDA program?
- ☐ What are the access terms of the STL offered by the publisher/ vendor/aggregator?
- ☐ What user activity will trigger an STL?
- ☐ Will you exclude publishers who do not allow STLs prior to purchase?
- ☐ Will you set a threshold price to exclude or go straight to purchase for titles that have an STL cost that is a high percentage of the list price?
- ☐ How many STLs will you allow, subject to any limits imposed by the publisher?
- ☐ What are the options for how many days an STL can last, and which will you allow?

- ☐ Can your library override STLs for individual titles, and go straight to purchase?
- ☐ How many STLs are allowed per day?
- ☐ What STL parameters can the library control or customize?
- ☐ Is there an option for allowing the user to choose the length of an STL at the point of use?

The experience of many libraries shows that most print books are only used a few times. Because of this, libraries using DDA find that adding an STL component to DDA saves money compared to going straight to purchase on the first triggered use. Before we started our DDA program, we did an analysis of our circulation statistics for a sample year's acquisitions and found that one year after purchase 66 percent had not circulated, 31 percent had circulated 1 to 3 times, and only 3 percent had circulated 4 or more times. This is consistent with other library circulation studies which find that small percentages of books account for the majority of loans, most books that circulate do so only a small number of times, and a significant percentage of books never circulate even after years on the shelf.

Most of the concerns about STLs are the same issues that apply to interlibrary loan. We don't really know how much use is actually made of most of the titles we borrow through interlibrary loan. Your library may end up paying for interlibrary loan service for a book that only has a few pages of interest to the user, or that the user decides is of limited value once it is in hand. Your library may also provide several interlibrary loans for the same title, only to end up purchasing it later, with no reimbursement for the cost of providing the prior loans.

You will need to decide the best STL length for your library, subject to your vendor's limitations. For ebrary titles, the standard options are 1 day or 7 day STLs, with up to 3 STLs prior to purchase, depending on the publisher. STLs of longer duration (up to 28 days) may be possible. If you have had a substantial number of e-books in your collection for several years, examining the use data will help inform your decision. Details of that use data may show the number of times individual titles are used. If you don't have a large set of e-book data, look at your own library's retrospective circulation data on print books to help you decide what might be an appropriate number of STLs. How many times does the same title get checked out? A one-day STL would maximize the number of users for a title through quick turnover, and if you have reason to believe that most people will use an e-book only once and not again, this length makes sense. A short STL may result in a single person using a book several days in a row and generating multiple successive STLs. However, looked at collectively for all DDA titles in a library's discovery pool, multiple short STLs are associated with lower overall costs. A seven-day STL would allow for longer use by an individual, and might prevent one person using up several STLs over several consecutive days. Another possible option, if your vendor allows it, is to let the individual user choose the length of the STL.

You will also need to decide how many STLs you will require prior to a purchase trigger. Libraries using DDA typically stipulate that there be anywhere from 0 to 9 or more STLs depending on their goals, though some vendors will restrict the number of STLs available on their platform. Requiring none or very few STLs encourages more titles to be purchased based on use, but will expend budgeted funds more quickly. Requiring a larger number of STLs prior to purchase will typically save money on the DDA program as a whole (though perhaps not on individual titles), and will lead to fewer permanent purchases. We choose three STLs based on an analysis of circulation of a sample of our print collection, and because we did not want to stop purchasing books altogether.

With STLs incorporated into a DDA program, the library pays a percentage of the cost of an e-book for each STL allowed. One additional use beyond the STLs allowed triggers a purchase at the full list cost of the e-book. The cost of STLs does not apply towards any future purchase of the title. Additional information about STL costs is included in the chapter on budgeting.

Verify the terms of STLs with your vendor(s). Some individual publishers do not allow STLs, even on aggregator platforms, so a single triggering event will result in a purchase at list price. This will typically result in higher spending, or at least faster spending. If you are using the STL option in an effort to slow or decrease spending, consider whether you want to exclude publishers that do not provide for STL, but weigh the cost-benefit of potentially excluding valuable content from your users. We decided to include all DDA eligible titles. Since the majority of the publishers we purchase from do provide STL, we have not found this to be a problem.

☐ Will you disclose to your users that there are records in your catalog for items you do not (yet) own?

☐ Might it concern your users or library funders to know that you are not actually buying these books for your library unless they get used, or unless they get used multiple times (in the case of STL)?

☐ Might it concern your users or library funders to know that
   STL use does not mean the book is a permanent part of the
   collection?

Some libraries have deliberately chosen not to disclose their DDA programs to
users so that they could monitor the results without unintentionally influencing
user behavior. The concern is that users will either avoid using DDA titles so as
not to cost the library money, or alternatively, will seek out and use DDA titles
just enough to make sure they are purchased and become part of the collection.
You may want to consider the value of being transparent from the start about
implementation of a DDA program, particularly with stakeholders to whom you
report administratively or who approve your acquisitions budget. Actively articu-
lating the intent and value of DDA to overall library operations may help avoid a
situation in which stakeholders misinterpret the goals of the program and how it
fits into the overall collections strategies of your library. DDA is being used by an
increasing number of libraries, but it is likely that most library users are unaware
of it. A few articles in the library literature have criticized DDA as undermining
the long-term building of local library collections, and you will want to be prepared to explain why and how your library is using DDA and how it helps you
serve your community.

   At our academic library, we decided that we would not keep DDA a secret. Many
faculty at our institution are active in recommending books for the library collection. Departments who are heavy users of monographs were informed of our plans
by their liaison librarians. We discussed our DDA pilot with our advisory committee, made up of faculty, prior to proceeding, and we reported on the implementation of DDA in multiple administrative reports, which are available to all college
faculty and administrative staff. Librarians also have mentioned DDA in various
committee meeting discussions related to library acquisitions and budgeting. We
also explain DDA and answer questions as they arise, sometimes in the context of
e-books in general. We did not attempt to advertise that we were using DDA to our
students, who are the majority of our library users. We felt in this way we could
maintain a level of administrative transparency without unduly influencing the
research behavior of our users to either favor or disfavor use of DDA titles. DDA
titles are identified in the detailed view of our public catalog records, which is helpful for technical services trouble-shooting and to help library staff avoid triggering a
use that is not necessary. Most users, however, would probably not recognize what
this means even if they chose to look at that view for a particular title.

- [ ] If you routinely buy titles on the recommendation of users, will you consider a DDA record to be a suitable substitute for a firm order?
- [ ] Will you want to and be able to "manually" add a title to your DDA discovery pool? If so, who will select individual DDA titles to add to your pool?

Libraries often purchase titles based on user recommendations, but adding them to your discovery pool is also an option. Consider whether your users are likely to actually use the library copy, or whether they are recommending titles they simply think are good books. Stetson University found that of 299 user-requested titles put into DDA, only 17 triggered an actual purchase (Dinkins, 2012). We have found that users who recommend a print title for our collection rarely check out the title. Some already own a personal copy of the title, which leads to their recommending it for the library collection. Some think a book sounds interesting based on a review they have read, but have no immediate intention to check out the book to read. By having the DDA discovery record available, the recommender can access the title if they really want to, but if they don't—and no one else does either—the library has not expended any funds.

By design, a profile will exclude titles deemed inappropriate for your collection based on preestablished criteria (publisher, genre, price, publication date, etc.). Even if you use a profile, you can decide to allow designated library staff to override the profile, and designate other titles for addition to your DDA discovery pool. Manual addition to your discovery pool is a possibility for titles that your profile did not include automatically. This involves determining whether an individual title is available as a DDA-eligible e-book, and working with your vendor to add it to your discovery pool. We allow librarians to designate any DDA-available title within the YBP Gobi system for addition to our DDA pool, even if it does not fit our existing profile. The titles are designated as "manual DDAs," and the MARC records will show up in our next profile-selected DDA batch for loading in our catalog. This is useful for titles that a librarian thinks look interesting, but is uncertain as to whether they would actually be used. The librarian can add it to the DDA pool, and if it is not used then no funds are spent. This is a less risky approach than buying a book that is peripheral to the collection. Librarians at our library also decided that unless a print copy is specifically requested, acquisitions staff should select an available DDA option as the default for all order requests submitted outside the YBP Gobi system. This allows us to include titles that were originally screened out by our profile parameters, but that are otherwise of potential interest to our users.

☐ What are your ownership rights once a purchase is triggered?

☐ Will your purchase preference be for single user copies or multiple user copies, or something in between?

☐ What other variations are available from the vendor(s)?

The most common model for e-books sold to libraries is the single user purchase option (SUPO) or the multiple simultaneous user purchase option (MUPO). It is usually much less expensive to provide SUPO, and that will likely be adequate for most titles. MUPO typically costs 150 percent of list price. You may be able to upgrade titles to MUPO later as needed if, for example, you discover a title is in high demand. Alternatively, if demand is high you can simply buy more copies, or buy one SUPO copy and supplement it with STLs for an initial period of high demand that you expect to taper off. Note that some publishers will not allow MUPO, and some will not allow STLs.

Other pricing and use models exist, so clarify with your vendors the specific models they offer. As of this writing EBL (now owned by ProQuest) offers a "Non-linear lending" model for most of the titles they offer. This allows multiple concurrent users for a copy of an e-book for up to 325 loans per year, or roughly one per day, per year. EBL also offers some titles with MUPO access, and a small number with a "textbook" model that limits the number of simultaneous users as well as the total number of loans per year. JSTOR offers e-books from multiple publishers with an unlimited user model. Some titles may be offered with a designated number of simultaneous users.

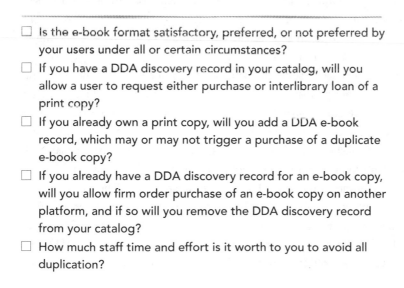

☐ Is the e-book format satisfactory, preferred, or not preferred by your users under all or certain circumstances?

☐ If you have a DDA discovery record in your catalog, will you allow a user to request either purchase or interlibrary loan of a print copy?

☐ If you already own a print copy, will you add a DDA e-book record, which may or may not trigger a purchase of a duplicate e-book copy?

☐ If you already have a DDA discovery record for an e-book copy, will you allow firm order purchase of an e-book copy on another platform, and if so will you remove the DDA discovery record from your catalog?

☐ How much staff time and effort is it worth to you to avoid all duplication?

All of the above scenarios increase costs for the library without adding new content. They are policy decisions for your library, based on weighing the benefits to users against the costs in both dollars and staff time. Allowing duplicates may increase convenience for your users. Some users will always prefer to read a print version of a book, and some users will sometimes prefer print depending on their purpose or the genre of the book. You may have, or wish to acquire, data or feedback from your local users regarding their format preferences. This can be applied to your DDA profile, allowing you to include or exclude specific subjects or genres depending on your users' preferences. If you don't already have a policy regarding format, you should consider establishing one. Good justifications can be made for either allowing duplication (optimal user satisfaction) or not allowing it (sustainable budget stewardship).

We decided that we would make the DDA discovery record (when available) the default for adding a title to our catalog, but for our faculty users we will purchase print duplicates on demand. This decision was a result of our awareness that the e-book format has not been fully embraced by all the users at our institution. At some point we may revisit this decision due to changes in user preferences as well as budgetary concerns, but we decided that satisfying our users' current format preferences was worth the occasional extra cost. We also decided that de-duping individual titles would create more work for our small technical services unit than it was worth. We have found that offering this flexibility has not resulted in a large number of duplicate print title purchases after all, and it is more than offset by the overall savings from using DDA. It is also consistent with our other policies of buying multiple print copies of a title under certain circumstances. Fortunately, requests for duplicate titles in an alternative format has not been such a common occurrence as to break our budget.

Also consider that while some publishers will simultaneously issue print and e-book versions, other publishers make the print version available first, and later make the e-book version available as much as eight weeks or more later. This is similar to the delay sometimes seen between issuance of a hardcover edition and the paperback. Publishers will also sometimes indicate that an e-book version will be made available, only to cancel publication in that format. The University of California's Irvine Libraries implemented a "time-sensitive buffer." Their DDA profile excluded any e-books not released within eight weeks of the print version. This helped them to avoid duplicating titles in two formats, and to avoid missing acquisition of titles that came out late, or never, in e-book format (Johnson 2011). The University of Colorado Boulder uses an "on hold for alternate edition" feature offered by their library service provider. This allows the library to set up detailed profiles for each subject, indicating a set time period to hold an order while waiting for the e-book version to become available. If the time expires with no e-book version, the print order is filled. Further profiling customization allows for specifying print-preferred circumstances, and for creating exceptions, such as requiring reference works to be ordered only in e-book format (Forzetting, Wiersma, and Eager 2012).

The University of Florida's Smathers Libraries worked with their book library services provider Ingram/Coutts to set up a DDA "preferred" approval plan. They identified publishers that routinely issued e-book versions within two months of print, and for those publishers the library stopped having print books automatically shipped, but instead waited to add an e-book discovery record. They achieved approximately $100,000 in savings by avoiding print duplication, and have been able to apply these funds to other collections initiatives (Carrico and Shelton 2012).

To minimize the purchase of duplicate titles, if not eliminate them altogether, you will need to have systems in place for identifying them. ISBNs are problematic for de-duping against owned print titles, because the numbers are not consistent for print and e-book, or even different print editions, of the same title, nor are they entered or coded consistently in catalog records. But they are typically the most practical means for automated batch elimination of most duplicates. A certain amount of duplication may be unavoidable, and you will want to weigh the staff time involved in weeding out duplicates against the potential savings.

At our library we decided that a small amount of duplication was acceptable when balanced against the overall increase in user access to a wide range of titles. We do take steps to minimize duplication. We use YBP's Gobi system, in which the record for the print edition of a book shows that an "alt-ed" (alternate edition) DDA record was sent to our library. Staff also check our catalog for duplicates before placing orders, but the practicality of this will depend on the volume of orders your library processes. Ingram also offers DDA services through their OASIS system. Your purchase history with your library services provider can be used to de-dupe a discovery pool. Also, if you are interested in loading retrospective records for DDA discovery, your library services provider may be able to compare your entire monograph holdings with your discovery pool, to eliminate duplicate titles even for books not acquired through your current library services provider. Ask your library services provider or other DDA vendor about the de-duping services they may offer, either at no additional cost or for additional one-time or ongoing fee. Such vendor-provided lists are useful if you are seeking to withdraw print copies duplicated by e-book holdings if, for example, you need shelf space in your library.

You can also make use of your DDA profile to minimize duplications. For example, you may want to screen out specific publishers or series from which you firm order e-books or have e-book packages. We have also found some government agency publications originally appeared in our DDA profile, even though electronic versions of their publications are available open access online.

☐ Will you allow DDA records to duplicate other e-book holdings?

☐ If you already own another e-book copy on a different platform (from a different vendor), will you add a DDA e-book record? For example, if you own a copy on the EBSCO platform, will you add a DDA discovery record for an ebrary copy?

☐ Will you de-dupe against large e-book collections you subscribe to or own?

If you are buying or subscribing to e-books in packages outside of your DDA program, you may end up with duplicate titles and records. If you already have paid access to an e-book, you won't want to pay again for a DDA-triggered use. Consider how likely this is to occur based on your overall e-book holdings. If your subscribed or purchased titles are on the same platform as your DDA program, the vendor may have a system in place that avoids you being charged for access made from a DDA discovery record. In that instance having a discovery record that duplicates another e-book record in your catalog will cause no harm financially. If you work with a library services provider, they may also be able to block your subscribed/purchased e-book packages from being included in your DDA profile and individual holdings. For individual e-book duplications that cannot be blocked by vendors, you should weigh the staff effort involved in hunting down and removing duplications against any potential cost savings. Liberty University's Falwell Library used a combination batch and manual review process to help identify duplicates of e-books and remove those titles from their discovery pool (Crane and Snyder 2013).

Some vendors will de-dupe for you if you supply title and ISBN lists (though ISBNs on e-books are problematic, as described above in the discussion on print duplication). OCLC numbers and titles are other possibilities, but also have problems. For example, OCLC numbers can appear in various MARC fields, and may not appear at all in vendor records. As for comparing lists by title, vendors that insert the series title before the title proper in their lists render this process difficult and unreliable. Depending on your integrated library system and level of systems support, you may be able to run scripts or batch processes to help identify duplicates. In some instances, your technical services staff may need to "hand weed" duplicate discovery records from your catalog, if you decide that the staff time is worth it to prevent an unnecessary trigger. Some libraries, including ours, have decided that a certain amount of duplication is acceptable relative to the work involved in hunting down every one.

- ☐ Which staff will be involved in day-to-day DDA operations?
- ☐ Will additional training be required?
- ☐ Who will manage the DDA program on an ongoing basis? Will you assign a dedicated project manager for DDA? Or will you have a team or committee approach?
- ☐ Will you work the various activities into your existing workflows and areas of responsibility (profiling, budgeting, licensing/contract review, ordering/purchasing, monitoring of spending, cataloging/catalog maintenance, assessment)?
- ☐ Which staff will take on new responsibilities? Do staff job descriptions need to be adjusted?

You should expect implementation of a DDA program to take extra time, especially during the initial planning, setup, and early weeks as new or revised workflows are being established. Catalog maintenance is ongoing and more complicated than that for purchases (see details in the cataloging chapter of this guide). All the work that applies to acquiring and managing e-books applies to DDA, plus the additional tasks described in this guide. That said, small libraries with only one or two technical services librarians, as well as large libraries with numerous technical services staff, are successfully implementing DDA programs.

There are many different technical services workflow approaches you can take. The University of Tennessee library decided that as the number of e-book acquisitions increased, the acquisitions and cataloging workload on their original two staff became unmanageable. They initially had a very thorough, and therefore labor-intensive, workflow which included entering each title in a local database and their electronic resource management system, in addition to adding each MARC record to the catalog. They also verified access to every e-book title, but were considering whether that was essential. As the volume of e-book titles grows, they are rethinking the necessity of all these steps and redundant records. Some of the ways they have streamlined their operations involve purchasing customized records from YBP, writing a local script to automate downloading of the records from YBP and automatically uploading them to their online catalog, and eliminating maintenance of a redundant local database of e-book acquisitions. Their large library includes a number of technical services departments that are involved, including legal, purchasing, e-resources and serials management, collections, library systems, and library business services (Hodge, Manoff, and Watson 2013).

Our library technical services unit is much smaller, with only 3.5 staff and 3 professionals who also provide public services. Despite having a small staff, we have found the effort to implement DDA to be worth it, as it has resulted in gains to user service through instant access to more titles, while achieving cost savings by not purchasing unused books. We make use of outsourcing by purchasing customized records from YBP and only spot-check URLs and access rather than checking every record. We have further moderated the impact on our staff by integrating DDA into existing workflows wherever possible. We also identified antiquated or low-priority technical services tasks that can be discontinued, and reassigned that staff time to support workflows related to e-books and other electronic resources. DDA for e-books acquisition has also reduced our print acquisitions and the attendant work of ordering and processing those, freeing staff time to manage DDA and e-books.

Optimizing User Access with DDA

Twenty years ago librarians grappled with the question of whether access could ever effectively substitute for ownership, due to the limits of delivery speed through interlibrary loan at that time. Today, DDA and growing e-book availability present a tremendous opportunity for libraries to make instant access to a large catalog of material available to users.

From a user standpoint, a link to a DDA title through the library is like any other e-book link. Most libraries load MARC records for individual DDA titles in their catalog, where they are discovered by the user—hence the term "discovery record." The user need not even be aware that the library has not (yet) paid anything for the title. If the user decides to connect to the title they are immediately presented with the full text, and from there will have a variety of choices depending on the platform and the options selected by the library. Typically the user may browse some of the pages for a certain amount of time before any charge is made to the library. Other options for the user include further online reading, checking it out for a period of time, downloading it to a mobile device for a certain period of time, and printing or copying portions of the text. If the e-book is being made available via a multiple user (MUPO) or Non-linear lending model, then additional users can read the book simultaneously.

Most of the user's activities will serve as "triggers" for a charge to the library. If the library has opted for one or more short-term loans (STLs) prior to purchase, the use may cost only a portion of the list price for the e-book. If the library has opted for the first use to trigger a purchase, or if all available STLs have already been exhausted, the use will trigger a charge to the library for the full list price. All the costs to the library will be invisible to the user. Nothing will notify the user that they have "triggered" a charge.

If your main reason for implementing DDA is to improve service to users, consider making a broad selection of DDA titles available. An increasing number of individual publishers are also offering some form of DDA, so this may be a desirable option for publishers with whom your library does a great deal of business. You can also set up a DDA program with an e-book aggregator that represents a wide range of relevant publishers and titles, such as ebrary or EBSCO. Using a library services provider intermediary, such as YBP or Ingram/Coutts, allows you to cast a wide net in making titles available across many subjects and genres via DDA. Your choice of vendors and specific DDA options will affect the level of service and convenience you are able to offer.

- ☐ Is the e-book interface (platform) user-friendly? Are reading, browsing, and searching within the full-text easy to do? Is pagination preserved and logical? Can it be read easily on large and small screens? Can text be resized or adjusted in other ways for ease of reading? Are there tools for bookmarking, highlighting, and annotating text? Are both black-and-white and color images of good quality? Can you jump to chapters from the table of contents and index entries? Is online help available, and is it actually helpful?
- ☐ Are any DRM restrictions acceptable?
- ☐ Is offline reading—downloading to a personal computer or mobile device—allowed and technically possible? Is special software required? Is the downloaded version easy to read and use?
- ☐ Is individual registration required, and if so, how is user privacy protected?
- ☐ Does the platform provide a satisfactory mobile device option(s)? What devices may be used? If there are mobile device apps, do they work well, and are they available for the devices most used by your users? Is the content compatible with e-book readers? Which ones, and are they the ones most used by your users?

Of course, these are not just DDA issues, but should be considered for any e-book offering. Shelton, Cataldo, and Buhler provide a helpful overview of e-book platforms from both a user and administrator perspective (2013).

Digital rights management refers to the technological means used to "lock down" online content to prevent copying, printing, downloading, or other manipulation of the digital file. DRM may also restrict access to those who own a particular type of e-book reading device. Overly restrictive DRM can be an impediment to routine uses of e-books for scholarly purposes. Different vendor platforms impose different levels of DRM restriction. E-books on the original publisher's platform may not have DRM restrictions. The degree of restriction on aggregator platforms varies. JSTOR, for example, offers e-books on its platform with no DRM restrictions, but offers a more limited selection of titles and publishers than other aggregators. It is not unusual to have some limitations, such as a limit to the number of pages from the e-book that can be printed. Examine the specific DRM restrictions when comparing vendors, but realize that you may need to accept some restrictions to obtain the titles that you want for your users.

☐ **Will you include DDA titles on new book lists or alerts for your users?**

Technically you don't yet own the titles, but by including them in the discovery pool you have made the decision that the title is of potential interest to your users. If the discovery records are included in your catalog, you may want to also include the titles on new book alert lists, since you are making the title easily available and will purchase it if it gets used. From a budgetary standpoint, you may be reticent to provide advertising of specific DDA titles, lest this trigger costs. However, if you don't want your users to actually use a DDA title, reconsider why you are even doing DDA. If you think a title thus advertised is highly likely to get use, then you should consider purchasing the title proactively. If you are not sure if it will get used or not, then DDA is appropriate.

☐ **Do you plan to monitor and deal with "turnaways"?**

If only one person at a time is permitted to use an e-book (SUPO option), then users will experience "turnaways" when they try to access a title already in use. Discuss with your vendor what activity may create a turnaway situation. For example, some e-book systems allow for "checking out" or downloading the single library "copy," which blocks other users from accessing the book during the checkout period. It may be possible for you to block downloading or extended checkout of a SUPO copy, or if you have simultaneous access to multiple copies, to allow down-loading/checkout of all but the last copy. Your vendor may provide administrative tools for you to manage these settings, so be sure to ask what options are available. It may also be possible for you to receive an e-mail alert when a turnaway occurs, and make a decision at that time. For example, we noticed that we were getting repeated turnaways on one specific title which led us to discover that there was a course assignment for which that book was especially relevant, so we purchased a MUPO copy for an additional one-time cost to meet the demand.

If you make policy decisions related to turnaways, you won't have to decide case-by-case what to do. For example, you may decide to automatically purchase a second copy or upgrade to a MUPO copy, assuming that is an option for the title. You should also find out if the turnaway message your users see can be custom-ized to make it more helpful and friendly to your users. Presenting an option to e-mail the library can provide a means to gather feedback from your users each time they experience a turnaway. Ask your vendor what options are available to ameliorate turnaways if that is a concern for your library. For example, ebrary has "extended access" options for turnaway prevention that you can customize in their administrative module. If a title is in use, you can allow short-term loans for an additional copy, or automatically upgrade to an available MUPO, for an additional percentage of the SUPO list price, or automatically purchase an additional SUPO copy subject to a price cap you specify.

Another approach is to simply not worry too much about occasional turnaways. In the world of print books, there are times when a user doesn't find what they want on the library shelves, and perhaps finds an alternative book instead, or comes back another time for the item. Especially if the loan period for your e-books is only one day, users may find the inconvenience of occasional turnaways to be minimal. Only you can decide if this is a serious issue for your library and your users. Consider ways you can make your users aware that library e-books are by definition a shared resource, and specific titles may occasionally be unavailable temporarily when in use by someone else.

- ☐ Will you restrict access to DDA discovery records to users affiliated with your library?
- ☐ Or will you also permit "walk-in" access to DDA titles, which will trigger a cost for the library?
- ☐ Are there licensing restrictions on access for guest or walk-in users?

If your intent is to use a DDA program to affordably expand access for your primary users, then you may want to consider whether you want guest or walk-in users to be able to access DDA discovery records. Will you allow guest users to trigger STLs or purchases of e-books? You may wish to consider your existing policies on providing interlibrary loan or inviting purchasing recommendations from guests in deciding whether or not DDA discovery records will be accessible to guests. If you decide not to allow DDA discovery by guest users, then you will need to determine policy or technological means to restrict this access. Access to discovery records can be restricted by requiring authentication through a proxy server or single sign-on authentication.

☐ Will you enable remote and mobile access for DDA records, and if so how will this be facilitated and managed technologically?

☐ Are there licensing restrictions regarding remote or off-site access?

Most vendor licenses will permit remote access for authenticated users, as that is one of the major benefits of e-books. Determine what options for remote and mobile access are available through your e-book vendor. One of the major advantages of the e-book format is remote and mobile use, including download-ing for offline reading on desktop or mobile devices. But enabling downloading may actually limit use by restricting access for a set period of time to the user that downloaded the title. Your library may be able to control the download or "checkout" period to control this, and you will need to determine your policy for this. Also, there may be more than one option for facilitating remote use. If your library has a proxy server, that is one option. A single sign-on system is another option. Determine which options will work with your vendor's system as well as with your local technological setup.

☐ How many access points will you make available (or will auto-matically be available) for your users to discover the DDA titles? Catalog, discovery layer, link resolver, guides, and title lists?

Most libraries using DDA load the MARC records in their catalog, despite the fact that the titles in the discovery pool are not yet owned and may never be owned. The very premise of DDA is to promote discovery and let the user decide if they want a title. If you don't put them in your catalog you are in a sense hiding the ball. Also, having the records in your catalog helps you avoid acquisitions duplication. For many libraries, the catalog also feeds records into their discovery layer, if they have one. However, if it is important to you that your catalog represent only those items that are already owned by your library, or if you have not been including e-books in your catalog, consider alternative ways to facilitate discovery of DDA titles.

A discovery layer (e.g., EDS, Summon, Primo) is another means of making DDA titles accessible to users. It is often possible to make the records directly viewable in your discovery layer, independent of whether or not you load them in your catalog. Discovery records, unlike MARC records, may be searchable at the chapter or full-text level. At our library, our catalog records are also included in our discovery layer, so we chose to load MARC records into our catalog and upload them to discovery layer as well. However, it is possible to include them only in a discovery record, and not also in your catalog. Work with your DDA e-book vendor and specific discovery layer vendor regarding your choices and the most efficient way to enable them.

Depending on the vendors you work with, DDA discovery records may automatically be cross-linked from other e-resources. For example, we have several article databases from ProQuest and have a DDA program with ebrary, also owned by ProQuest. ProQuest inserts links in the databases to related ebrary e-book records to which our library has access. From the vendor's point of view, this promotes more use of their e-books and possibly more DDA triggers. But our library also views it as a value for our users, who see links to relevant content they might not otherwise discover on their own.

Users may also end up finding their way to your DDA records via web searches, or because looking at one title on a vendor's platform leads them to other titles on that same platform. A study at Kent State libraries found that 28 percent of their e-book use came from outside their catalog (Downey et al. 2014).

You should also think about whether or not you want to include discovery records in any guides or special title lists your library makes available. For example, if you regularly produce a "new book list," do you want to include only purchased titles, or also newly available DDA titles?

☐ How will DDA affect your interlibrary loan service use and costs? Will DDA reduce your need to borrow from other libraries on behalf of your users?

☐ Is interlibrary loan to other libraries allowed following the purchase of an e-book through DDA, and under what terms?

Since DDA allows instant access to titles not owned by your library, it may be thought of as an alternative to traditional interlibrary loan. This is particularly true if your DDA program incorporates STLs. Reports from some libraries using DDA indicate that their interlibrary borrowing has gone down significantly, while other libraries report no change.

On the flip side, licensing terms that allow lending of owned titles to other libraries is not just a DDA question, but is such an important long-term e-book question for libraries that it bears mention here. To the extent that DDA may become a significant part of library acquisitions strategies, the long-term impact on interlibrary loan networks should be considered. Vendors are aware of this concern, and language concerning allowable interlibrary loan shows up in some e-book contracts. Libraries should raise this issue during discussions of licensing terms.

Budgeting for DDA

Early concerns about unexpected runaway costs have faded as DDA management tools provided by vendors have matured. In the early days of DDA libraries experimented with loading large sets of discovery records simply because they were available, and with minimal efforts at profiling. The free browsing periods prior to triggering were also much less generous in early DDA programs. Libraries no longer report unanticipated cost overruns as a common problem, and those using DDA as part of overall collections strategies are actually experiencing savings.

In thinking about cost concerns, compare the risks of DDA expenditures to the risk of advance purchasing books that are never used, which is arguably a substantial and well-documented waste of collection dollars. We have not had a problem with rapid spending at our library, and we believe this is because we also have large subscription e-book packages (which bear an annual, fixed, predictable cost), and we also enable short-term loans prior to purchase, when possible.

There are several things you need to consider in order to thoughtfully develop a DDA program for your library: what your goals and priorities are, information about your users and their library use habits, and information about your existing collection. While there is no magic formula, by using your local information and the experience of other libraries, you can shape a local DDA program that is highly likely to be successful in meeting your goals and staying within budget.

There are multiple, established methods for balancing increased user access with DDA cost control. These include carefully developing your discovery pool profile using subject and non-subject parameters, STLs, coupling DDA with subscription e-book packages, and proactive purchasing of high-use e-books individually or in packages.

While these have been discussed somewhat in earlier chapters, in this chapter the focus will be on incorporating DDA into the library acquisitions budget.

Keep in mind that an e-book DDA program alone will not be a panacea for dealing with a tight budget. Many books that libraries might wish to acquire are not made available as e-books at all. YBP Library Services reports that of all the titles they handled from July 2012 through March 2013, only 42 percent were published in e-book format within eight weeks of the print publication (Baker and Breaux 2013). Publishers will allow DDA for only a subset of titles made available in e-book format, and for those e-books allowed as DDAs, STL options may not be allowed, resulting in the first use triggering a purchase at list price.

☐ How do your collection goals balance temporary access with permanent ownership of books?
☐ How important is it to maintain access throughout your budget year to any DDA discovery titles loaded in your catalog or other access points?

If it is an important goal for your library to use DDA to help build your permanent collection, then set up your program to drive purchases, rather than minimize costs. You can develop a profile, using vendor tools, to choose titles for your DDA discovery pool that you would consider appropriate acquisitions for your library. By not enabling STLs, or enabling very few, use of titles will be more likely to trigger a purchase and addition to your collection, although your overall DDA costs will be higher, since most titles are only used a few times. Studies from academic libraries have found that e-books purchased via DDA have a relatively high rate of future use compared to librarian-selected titles, making DDA an effective tool for collection building.

If funds allotted for DDA are exhausted more quickly than anticipated, despite your best planning efforts, there is always the option to "turn off" the DDA program at any time, and either suppress or remove unused DDA discovery records from the catalog and other access points. Some libraries feel that once they have loaded a set of discovery records into their catalog they must maintain them there throughout the fiscal year, because users will have come to expect them. If this is a concern for your library, then you may want to consider adding DDA discovery records gradually to your catalog, rather than loading a large retrospective set of records all at once. In this way you can wade slowly into DDA while monitoring local use, and hold back on adding records until you see if use exceeds what you anticipated.

☐ How many e-books do you already have in your collection from sources other than DDA?

☐ How heavily used are your existing e-book collections?

☐ What will be the proportion of DDA titles to other e-books? To your entire holdings?

The answers to these questions may predict how much use you are likely to see for your DDA e-book titles. If the DDA discovery records added to your catalog will make up a relatively small proportion of your other e-book and print collections, then it is likely you will see less use of DDA titles. Our library has experienced slow and steady use of our DDA titles. We couple our DDA program with large e-book subscription packages and e-books we have firm-ordered. As a result, our DDA discovery records represent less than 10 percent of available e-book titles in our catalog. Use of our two large subscription e-book packages (one from the same vendor as our DDA titles) has been very high, and because we pay a flat rate for the e-book collection subscriptions, it is easy to budget for them. In proportion to the collection of all the e-book titles we make available, the DDA titles are a pro-verbial drop in the bucket, but they are steadily used and thus provide a valuable supplement to our other acquisitions strategies. Although use of the subscription e-book titles never results in purchases, the vendor provides lists of titles used, and we could choose to firm order high-use titles if we desired to add them to our permanent collection.

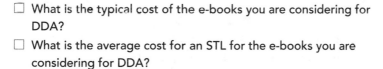

☐ What is the typical cost of the e-books you are considering for DDA?

☐ What is the average cost for an STL for the e-books you are considering for DDA?

E-book versions of print books may cost less, the same, or more than the print version. Also, e-books that allow more than one simultaneous user are more expensive. Find out from your vendor the average, median, and range in price for the titles you are considering for DDA, as well as STL costs. Through profiling you can put a cap on the cost of included titles as well as STLs. Vendors can provide cost data. If you work with a library service provider for the bulk of your acquisitions, they have a great many details about your collection building. They can be a good source for standard and custom reports on your historical spending that can help you with budget projections.

- ☐ What is the size of your user population?
- ☐ If you have significant e-book collections already, how much are they used?
- ☐ What is the use of your collection as a whole (circulation data)?
- ☐ What proportion of DDA discovery records will be in your catalog relative to the total number of records?
- ☐ What proportion of DDA discovery records will be in your library catalog relative to the total number of e-books you have available?
- ☐ How popular are e-books as a format with your users? Are they likely to limit to that format in your catalog?

Gathering and studying information about the demographic makeup of your user population and their library use habits will be useful in planning your DDA program setup. A large population that actively uses many library books per person each year, and that actively uses e-books in particular, necessitates a larger amount budgeted for DDA. This requires a more carefully regulated and more closely monitored DDA program in order to stay within the library budget. Reports from smaller academic libraries indicate that surprisingly few titles trigger STLs or purchases through DDA. Large universities have had different experiences and resulting costs. A library that supports a commuter population or distance education students may predict higher use of e-books than a smaller library with a localized population that uses more of a mix of print and e-books.

- ☐ Where will the money for your DDA program come from?
- ☐ How much money do you want to dedicate to your DDA program?
- ☐ Is your DDA program intended to be a small experiment or pilot?
- ☐ Is DDA only one of several strategies for building your book collection?

Most libraries implementing DDA dedicate a portion of their acquisitions funds. If you are going to run a "pilot" DDA program, you may be able to or want to use gift money, or request a special one-time budget appropriation for that purpose. Some libraries are part of larger institutions that provide "innovation" grants or other special monies that can be applied for. Even if you run a pilot, think ahead to how you could continue funding the program if you decide that it is successful. We saw DDA as fitting into our overall strategy for holding the line on book budget increases, so we allotted a portion of our regular book budget for our pilot. Now that DDA has become part of our an ongoing collection building strategy, our library simply pays for DDA purchases out of our general book budget as we would for a monograph acquired via any other means. We do not keep a separate budget line or target for DDA acquisitions.

You have the ultimate control over how much you spend on DDA. You decide how much money you want to allocate, and work with your chosen vendor(s) to put systems in place to halt triggering of purchases beyond your budgeted amount. This is really no different than the experience many libraries have had, at times, of expending their book budget prior to the end of a fiscal year and temporarily halting additional print book orders. You can avoid budgetary problems simply by monitoring the pace of spending throughout your fiscal year.

Deciding how much money to allot to a new DDA program is the most difficult question, because you may feel that a crystal ball is needed to predict spending based on future user behavior. Several approaches are possible. If you already have e-books in your collection, looking at usage statistics at the title level will give you an idea of how many titles, and what proportion of e-book titles, are used and how often each is used. You can then extrapolate from this data to estimate the use you might see from titles in a DDA discovery pool. If you do not have a substantial number of e-books, then you can make the same estimates based on circulation data for print monographs. The results will be less predictive, though, particularly if you allow long print book loan periods that limit potential turnover. In deciding how much money to allot for DDA, consider the cost of the e-book format compared to print. An e-book for the library market may be less, the same, or more costly than the same book in print. Usually it will be the same cost or somewhat more than the price of the hardcover print edition for a single-use (SUPO) copy, although some titles cost substantially more in e-book format. Multiple use copies (MUPO) will cost more than SUPO copies, but actual costs vary widely depending on the publisher, the e-book platform, and the specific pricing model.

A less scientific, but easier approach, is to pick a somewhat arbitrary amount with which you are willing to experiment for a pilot, knowing that whatever amount is spent is providing content that your users actually want. You might, for

39

example, decide on a percentage of your book budget, or simply a round number that doesn't seem too risky to your institution. When the money runs out, you can end your initial pilot and analyze the data to estimate a future amount to dedicate to DDA, if you decide to continue with it. This is basically the approach we took for our first DDA pilot. We initially dedicated approximately $4,000 with uncertainty as to how long it would last. Because we have a relatively small user population we guessed that the funds would be sufficient. Triggers happened slowly and steadily, such that our initial dedicated amount lasted approximately six months. We were prepared in advance to either cut off the pilot or allot more funds from our general book fund, if the triggered costs exceeded our initial budgeted amount. Because DDA was meeting our goals, we opted to assign more money from our book fund to the program. Large university libraries have reported dedicating $50,000 to $200,000 to their initial DDA programs.

☐ What are the budget restrictions under which you operate?

☐ Are you working from an overall acquisitions budget, with flexible ability to reallocate across lines (for serials, books, etc.)? Or do you have more rigid, separate acquisitions budget lines?

☐ Is it essential or important to you to distribute spending for monographs according to some formula across subjects or disciplines (however you define those)?

☐ How important is it to avoid cost overruns of any magnitude for DDA? If the funds you initially allot for DDA are expended before the end of your budget cycle, will you be able to replenish them?

☐ If you will pay via a deposit account, will the money roll over if not spent in a certain period of time, or is it a "use it or lose it" commitment of funds? Will you earn interest on the deposited amount, or get a discount in lieu of interest?

☐ What other fees will your vendors charge?

DDA takes away the ability to predetermine how much will be spent in a specific subject area, because you don't know in advance which e-books in which disciplines will trigger purchases. Our DDA profile covers a wide range of subject areas, since we serve a liberal arts institution. We have found that our DDA purchases are remarkably well distributed across disciplines, based on LC classification number. We no longer maintain separate subject funds, having instead a single "book" fund. Our DDA program arguably does a better job of evenly distributing purchases across disciplines than our typical reliance on faculty recommendations and librarian selections, because some faculty and librarians are much more active selectors than others at our institution. DDA also seems to do a better job of adding interdisciplinary titles to our collection, which might otherwise be missed by selectors/recommenders focusing on defined or traditional subject areas. Other libraries have similarly found that the spread of DDA purchases across disciplines has been reasonably well balanced across subjects. Even if such balance was not achieved, consider whether or not there is a real advantage for your users in attempting to achieve a "balanced" collection. If you are acquiring books based on some notion of "fairness" across subjects, but books in some of those subject areas are not used, what have you gained for your users and at what cost?

Your chosen vendor may require a particular payment method, or it may be negotiable. Most typical is a deposit account. This can actually benefit the library from a budgeting and invoice-processing perspective, depending on how your institutional financial operations deal with deposit accounts. You pay a set amount to the vendor up-front from your current fiscal year budget, and the funds will be drawn down automatically as titles are triggered. There is no need to process individual invoices, and no need to wait for order processing or to rush orders in at the end of a fiscal year to meet a target date. Alternative to actually paying out funds in advance is to "pledge" a set amount which you commit to spend over a set period of time, via a formal contract. As purchases are triggered the library is invoiced. The purpose of specifying an amount up-front, via deposit or pledge, is to limit the chance of cost overruns. You can monitor triggered spending, and as you approach the amount agreed on, you can decide to either commit more funds or to suspend the DDA program. The vendor should provide an alert, or at least an administrative reporting function, so that you can monitor spending closely as you approach the limit set. This allows you to stay within budget.

For either of these methods, the ideal is to negotiate the "rollover" of any undisbursed funds or pledged amount to future fiscal periods or years, especially during the first year of your program. You may be surprised to find that your users trigger fewer purchases than anticipated, and you certainly do not want to either lose unspent money or be forced to spend it abruptly. Another possibility is a simple pay-as-you-go approach, with the library invoiced for each STL or purchase as it occurs. Some vendors will allow conversion to pay-as-you-go after an initial period with a deposit account.

In addition to the actual cost of STLs and triggered e-book purchases, some vendors will charge DDA service administration fees or additional fees for opt-in services such as MARC record customization. Discovery records may be made available at no cost, but there is often a fee for point-of-invoice records. There may also be a platform or hosting fee for the e-book reader software. Find out up-front from any vendors you work with what additional fees may apply. Any costs that would apply to your routine e-book purchases, such as authority processing, will also apply to titles purchased via DDA.

☐ If you are tracking acquisitions using a variety of funds in your ordering and accounting system, what fund(s) will be assigned to titles purchased through DDA?

☐ Will you use a separate DDA fund, or use dollars from your primary "book" fund(s)?

☐ Will you pay for one or more "short-term loans" prior to triggering a purchase? If so, what funds will you use to pay for STLs, since you will not own the item?

☐ What do you want to track for both budgeting and overall assessment purposes?

Consider how you will be evaluating your DDA program in conjunction with how you plan to track spending. Fund tracking may be one way of evaluating use and cost-effectiveness, and if you plan to do that sort of analysis you will want to set up one or more separate funds in advance for DDA purchases. Take into account the practicality of tracking and managing whatever funds you set up. Creating a single, separate DDA fund can be worthwhile and easy to track, while setting up a separate DDA fund for each of many individual subject funds will double the tracking and management you need to do. If not necessary for assessment or to fulfill institutional accounting requirements, consider limiting the number of new funds you create. Also, if you lack the ability to move expenditures between budget lines, having a separate, dedicated DDA account or fund can work against you if you want to reallocate any unspent funds late in your fiscal year.

At our library we decided to assign any triggered purchases to our single "book" fund, since at that point the library owns the e-book. Expenditures exclusively for our DDA program can easily be determined using reports from our DDA aggregator, so our fund accounting system is not needed for this purpose. Alternatively, if you have a dedicated "e-book" fund you may want DDA e-book purchases included there.

If your library has multiple librarians acting as subject-selectors who are individually responsible for separate funds, discuss how DDA will either work in conjunction with your existing selection system, or rethink your system. Librarians responsible for selecting may be reluctant to give up control of collection building by having the dollars they spend reallocated to DDA. For this reason, you may wish to fund your DDA program, at least initially, from sources other than subject-selector funds, perhaps a "general" fund. Other options are to use a proportion of each selector's fund for DDA, or to "charge" DDA purchases to relevant subject funds after the fact, or with selector approval. In any case, librarian-selector expertise can be engaged during the DDA profile creation phase. If done well, the DDA profile in essence captures the collection development goals of the library by creating a discovery pool of only those titles that the library would consider buying anyway, if sufficient funds were available. Depending on the other duties the librarians have, they may find that the time freed from title-by-title selection allows them to better meet their other areas of responsibility such as teaching, reference services, and outreach.

You may want to consider alternative funds for tracking STL charges, since these expenditures do not result in ownership. If you are primarily interested in tracking all expenditures for your DDA program as a whole, include STL charges in the same DDA fund that you use for purchases. You should still make sure you have some means of separating out STL charges, however, perhaps by using vendor reports, because tweaking the number of STLs prior to purchase is a key tool for balancing access and ownership as well as overall DDA costs. At our library we decided to assign STL charges to the fund we use to track payments for interlibrary loan or "pay-per-view" provision of information for users, since the library gains no permanent ownership from the transaction. This allows us to track these with other access costs, separate from purchases that are added to the library collection. We asked our library service provider to give us separate invoices for DDA purchases and STL charges to make this accounting easier. Order information is included with the point-of-purchase MARC records, and is used to generate an order record in our acquisitions system.

☐ What tools are available through your vendor to control costs, both at the program level and at the individual STL and purchase level? For example, what kinds of alerts can the vendor provide when there are triggers, or when you approach thresholds of overall spending?

☐ What will be the list price cap (if any) for individual titles added to your DDA pool?

☐ Will you set a program limit or cap, with your vendor, on the amount to be spent for your overall DDA costs?

☐ What are the implications for your acquisitions budget as a whole if you don't spend all the money you budgeted for DDA?

☐ If you run out of money allocated for DDA purchases before the end of your fiscal period, will you add more funds, or will you suspend for the budget year? What is your plan for monitoring expenditures? Who will do the monitoring, and how often?

Early reports from libraries experimenting with e-book DDA ranged from quickly running out of funds dedicated to DDA due to fast triggering of purchases, to having low and steady triggering of DDA purchases such that dedicated funds lasted. Concerns about runaway costs have diminished greatly as libraries have taken advantage of profiling tools and STL options to tweak their DDA programs, and as trigger thresholds have become more reasonable. When choosing publishers or vendors to work with, you should carefully scrutinize the trigger criteria, being mindful of the amount of "free" browsing that is allowed before a use triggers an STL or purchase. The publisher/aggregator/vendor definition of STL and purchase triggers is critical in determining how quickly money is spent. Your vendor should provide you with the option of receiving alerts when DDA uses are triggered, and to generate on-demand reports to monitor DDA uses and expenditures.

Setting a list price cap will prevent sticker shock from a user triggering the purchase of a very high-priced item, such as an online encyclopedia. If you allow for manually adding titles to your DDA pool, you can override the price cap for special circumstances. In choosing a price cap, be sure to consider the average cost of titles from the publishers likely to be of interest to your user population. A price cap set too low might overly exclude a lot of valuable content, decreasing the service value of your DDA program. However, if you don't set a price cap, you are assuming a great risk that you will very quickly run through your DDA budget. Note that an overall cap on list price is applied to the list price of the e-book at the time it goes in your discovery pool, and there is a possibility that a publisher might increase the price of individual titles after they are already in your discovery pool.

Use of one or more STLs prior to purchase can considerably slow spending by minimizing the expense of providing access to titles that are used only a few times. If you are using a library services provider or aggregator, your DDA program will likely include numerous publishers, each of whom sets different allowances and costs for STLs. For budgeting, one of the most useful vendor tools is the ability to control the number and price of STLs. STL costs vary by publisher, and typically range from 10 to 50 percent of list price. The actual STL cost depends on the publisher and the length of the STL. A 28-day STL can run as high as 85 percent of list price. Ask your vendor about tools to block certain publishers based on STL terms, to build a separate profile for publishers based on STL terms, or to disallow STLs that exceed a certain percentage of title list price. It is important to note that any STL amounts paid do *not* apply to future purchase. So if an e-book has a list price of $30 with an STL of 33 percent, three STLs will total the cost of one purchase, and a subsequent purchase will still cost the full list amount. So three STLs followed by a fourth purchase trigger will total $60, or 200 percent of the list price. However, as previously stated, few books see four uses, so it still can make budgetary sense to use this model overall. STLs allow your library to offer instant access to many more titles than you could if you purchased every title on the first use. If there are e-books for which you can reasonably anticipate a lot of use (for example, the latest hot novel or a book central to your college curriculum), then you might consider buying one or more copies up-front rather than through DDA with STL.

Still, there are times when STLs will not make sense for individual titles already in your discovery pool. Ask your vendor if you have the ability to override STLs and go straight to a purchase for individual titles. You may want to do this if you are certain you want to own the title, or if you suspect that use for a particular title will be high enough to eventually trigger a purchase, and you want to avoid STL costs prior to purchase. Books reviewed widely in the media, or books used to support an academic course may predictably generate a lot of use. You will need to decide if you have an efficient way to monitor these events and override the STLs. Consider the cost-benefit of savings on STLs relative to the staff time cost needed for close monitoring.

As a last resort, you can be prepared to suspend DDA temporarily if your budget limit for the fiscal year is approached. If controlling your budget is your main driver, you may also want to use DDA as part of a larger strategic approach to providing access to a wide array of titles. For example, you can couple DDA for individual titles with subscription e-book collections at a flat, predictable rate for the most highly used titles. You will need to decide how serious a service concern it would be for your library to cut off access to the discovery pool abruptly (and shadow or remove the records from your catalog). Keep in mind that you don't actually own these books yet, so you are not taking away actual content from your collection or your users. You can still fill requests as you would any other title you don't own, such as through interlibrary loan or purchase. You can ameliorate having the problem in future years by adjusting your DDA program and allocating more funds, adding or adjusting the number of STLs prior to purchase, or adjusting your profile in various ways. Your vendor may also provide an automated means of cutting off your DDA program when a specified spending limit is reached. Some vendors will do this if you exceed the amount in your deposit account, or if you exceed the amount you "pledged" to spend. If you have set a cap for total spending, access to e-books from all discovery records will be shut off, and any users trying to connect to those titles will be denied access. This is one of the most important circumstances to avoid. Vendors are also beginning to offer the option of DDA without any spending cap, so there is no risk of losing access abruptly. To avoid either abrupt cutoff of service associated with spending caps, or the risk of cost overruns if you have no spending cap, you will want to assign one or more staff to monitor spending and trigger alerts and reports on a routine basis.

It is also possible that you will end up under-spending your DDA budget. Especially in the first year of a DDA program, it can be difficult to predict the costs that will be triggered by a specific user population, so you may find that you actually spend quite a bit less on DDA then you anticipated. If your library has a use-it-or-lose-it budget, unspent DDA funds may represent a lost opportunity to use the money for other acquisitions. For this reason, you may not want to begin a DDA program late in your fiscal year, and you should monitor DDA spending from the start so that you will have more time to adjust to an unexpected underuse of your discovery pool titles. If your DDA funds are paid from general or subject specific book funds, you will have time to spend the money on other materials.

Cataloging Aspects of DDA

Kirk Doran

☐ What is the purpose of your library's catalog?
☐ What is your library's philosophy regarding the catalog's purpose and contents?
☐ Will you include DDA discovery records in your catalog?

To catalog or not to catalog DDA titles? It is tempting to answer this question with a succinct "no" and move on. It would be simpler to skip the ins and outs of adding DDA discovery records to the catalog, and in the short term, easier on your technical services staff. Apart from making life temporarily easier, some other valid points can be made about *not* cataloging DDA discovery records. Let's address them briefly before dismissing them out of hand.

If you believe the purpose of a local catalog is to represent what you *own*, then DDA *discovery* records don't belong there, only DDA *point-of-invoice* records. By eliminating DDA discovery records, rentals, and for that matter, subscriptions without perpetuity rights, your catalog will project a clear picture of in-hand, in-house acquisitions only. This may be desirable to some constituents of the library's community. It will also make the catalog a cleaner source of statistics on the library's current holdings and growth in terms of *purchases*.

Kirk Doran is the technical services librarian at Dickinson College, where he has worked for the past fifteen years. His primary responsibilities are managing the SirsiDynix Symphony cataloging module, supervising team workflow, and performing original cataloging.

There is also the benefit of clutter control. Some users feel increasingly over-whelmed by their search results in the catalog. This can be an ironic side effect of a well-funded acquisitions budget. Particularly if they are expecting a catalog of mostly print books, users will be perplexed when a simple search retrieves such a heavy dose of e-books. Recurring batch loads of DDA discovery records populate an increasing proportion of search results. In integrated library systems sorted by "last in, first out," freshly introduced DDA records appear at the top of keyword search results. In that sense, they are competing with traditional new acquisitions for the attention of the user. DDA records can similarly crowd automatically gener-ated lists of new materials based on date cataloged.

Finally, some users, such as faculty members at an academic library, have a long-term stake in the library's collection. For example, while preparing for a class, a professor may scour the catalog for relevant materials, and conclude their class is well supported. Without knowing which of the materials they found were actually only DDA discovery records, they might be surprised to learn those records could disappear one day if not used. Faculty members might therefore prefer to browse DDA titles in a separate database, using it as a selection tool. Then they could trust the catalog to represent what they perceive as the *real* collection.

Some of the arguments above are philosophical. The nature and purpose of a library catalog, for example, is up for debate. Other reasons not to catalog DDA items are more practical, and some of these have practical and simple solutions. In more than one case, stumbling blocks can be removed by abandoning an all-or-nothing approach. The trickier aspects require creative thinking, experimentation, and a little courage. The best resolutions for all these issues will come from a flex-ible workflow behind the scenes and clear communication to the public out front.

Returning to our question "to catalog or not to catalog DDA titles," our answer was "yes," and details on methods are discussed in this chapter. Access vs. owner-ship is not a new topic in libraries, and the catalog has been representing both for years. For example, public libraries temporarily catalog rentals and multiple copies of best sellers, and academic libraries catalog personal items on reserve and subscriptions without long-term retention. Even among outright purchases, the concept of ownership is stretched. With formats such as online e-books and stream-ing media, nothing physical actually resides in the building. Instead of a physi-cal acquisition, it is the right to access a remote digital source that is purchased. Finally, one may question what constitutes a *permanent* acquisition. Suppose the faculty member above had found her course well supported by purchased print books in the collection. If they remain unused over time, are they not also at risk of being withdrawn?

The catalog is already representing much more than physical acquisitions. In terms of permanence, it includes materials with varying lifespans, some much longer than others, but perhaps few truly permanent. In catalogs that do not hide them from the public, order records indicate the most recent acquisitions before they are actually available. They merely alert people that access, whether tangible or digital, is coming soon. Following this logic a step further, it makes sense that the catalog should also represent *potential* acquisitions. And in the case of a DDA discovery title, access is immediate. Its status as "not quite purchased yet" is unknown to the user. Even if the record is flagged and tagged to beat the band, its unique status will probably go unnoticed by most people.

As to the question of clutter, this may well be a futile struggle, given that DDA records are only one small segment of information overload. But certain workflow decisions and management of files can alleviate, if not eliminate, the concerns previously listed.

☐ Which staff will be responsible for your DDA cataloging work? Will it be the responsibility of one person, or a team?

As described in this chapter and in the chapter on administration and management, there are many technical services tasks and activities that require ongoing attention and skill. Even larger libraries that take a team approach need to designate a primary contact for vendor notices regarding MARC record availability, changes, and withdrawals.

☐ Will you include discovery records on "new acquisitions" lists?

Consider whether or not to include DDA discovery records in automatically generated new books lists. Here again, they will overpopulate the lists immediately following the importation of large files. You could argue they are not new acquisitions, and don't really belong on the list at all. One way to exclude them is to leave the "date cataloged" set to blank or never, since the date cataloged is what captures titles for new acquisitions lists. As potential acquisitions, though, perhaps they deserve a list of their own. This will segregate them from other newly available resources, but that may make sense if you see their presence as competing with print and other non-DDA records. Conversely, if you want to promote their use, you could use both the date of loading and the new acquisition list to market your DDA program. A news announcement could highlight new DDA records on the first day of every month, or every Monday, or whenever new discovery records are added. Similarly, seeding your new books list with DDA records will expose them to all users who like to check your new acquisitions regularly. Given that there is no physical book display for DDA titles, or any e-book for that matter, why not promote them doubly? Include them in new acquisitions lists and in a list all their own.

☐ **If you have a discovery layer, will you include DDA discovery records in it?**

Your decision to include DDA discovery records in your discovery layer (e.g., Summon, EBSCO Discovery Service, Primo) will most likely mirror your decision to include them in the catalog at all. In other words, if your discovery layer includes an exact copy of your catalog, then it will include or exclude DDA discovery records according to your local decision to catalog them. Depending on your DDA vendor and discovery layer, you may be able to include DDA discovery records as a database, apart from your catalog. Be aware that including discovery records in both the catalog and the discovery layer may increase clutter with duplicate records. However, access through your discovery layer does provide an alternative way to market and expose the records to users, possibly with the added value of full text indexing. Your decision will be influenced by the extent to which your users are more likely to use your discovery layer than your catalog.

☐ **What source will you use for your discovery records?**
☐ **How will you coordinate loading of discovery records with your other cataloging workflows?**

You will have choices of where to obtain your discovery records, and your decisions will affect the issues described here. Records should be available from the publisher, e-book aggregator, your library services provider, or from the bibliographic utility you use, such as OCLC. Consider cost of records, their quality, convenience of their integration into your existing workflows, timeliness of availability, and customization options available.

☐ How often will you add DDA discovery records, and how many records will you load at one time, considering the impact on users of your catalog?

Since cataloging DDA discovery records individually is impractical, it can be assumed that we are talking about batch cataloging, that is, loading files of multiple records into the local integrated library system. How often this is done and the number of records added each time is going to impact the public catalog. Before worrying about the best source of MARC records and the best way to edit them, it is worth thinking through all the ramifications of loading DDA discovery records at all. This can be expressed by the "equation" $f \times q = e$, where f = the frequency of loading records, q = the quantity of records in each file loaded, and e = the effect on the catalog for the user.

As mentioned above, in systems where the default sort is "last in, first out," the recently added records are going to appear highest in the list of results from any keyword search. Therefore, adding one file of 500 records on the first of each month is going to have a significant and immediate influence on search results. Assuming the 500 titles cover a variety of topics relevant to users' research needs, their search results are going to have a higher percentage of DDA records on the first of the month, and the days immediately following. This percentage will drop over the next thirty days, as other non-DDA cataloging is added to the system. Then on the first of the next month the cycle will repeat. The exact proportion of DDA records to non-DDA records will depend on the number in each category and when they are loaded. How many of each will appear at the top of search results lists will also vary depending on the keywords entered by the user. A strictly mathematical equation would only hold true for null searches. And if your catalog allows an "empty" search, this is an easy way to test the ratio regardless of topic. For example, a search in SirsiDynix Symphony on #0 allows one to browse the most recent additions to the catalog regardless of topic or format. In the above scenario, the search results for a null search immediately following the record load would be 100 percent DDA discovery records for the first 500 results. Each day following, as other records are added, the percentage of DDA records among the first 500 results would drop. And this would continue until the next DDA batch load.

This bulge in DDA records is not necessarily a bad thing, but it may have some interesting effects. We know that many people tend to select results from the first screen only of a results list. We also know, in the case of periodicals certainly, that they will select online sources over print. We don't know yet if this second preference will hold true with e-books. But if the first principle applies, and the first screen is predominantly DDA records, then we can expect to see an increased use of DDA sources, and a decreased use of other sources in the catalog. Again, this effect will decrease over time until the next record load. If you think of DDA records as competing with non-DDA records for the attention of users, you can smooth out their influence by loading records more frequently and in smaller batches. Another option would be to re-index your catalog when you load large DDA batches, so those records don't dominate the first screen(s) of search results. And finally, this may not be an issue in library catalogs where the indexing of new records functions differently from last in, first out.

☐ How often will you add DDA discovery records, and how many records will you load at one time, considering the impact on your technical services staff?

Regardless of the source of MARC records, you will need to decide on the frequency and quantity of file loading that fits best with your staffing and existing workflows. Even if files are provided from a vendor weekly, they can be stored, merged, and loaded less frequently, or split into smaller batches and loaded more frequently. The most unobtrusive way to add DDA records would be either to load very small files every day, or to re-index the catalog after less frequent but larger loads. Neither of these extremes may be possible depending on the demands on staff and server time. And such an approach is probably not necessary; weekly loads, with their admitted effect on search results, will probably work fine.

DDA discovery record loads will also impact the routine file handling that technical services regularly does for all new cataloging. This includes batch uploads to discovery layers, file transfers to authority processing vendors, batch uploads to OCLC to set WorldCat holdings, and running statistical reports.

☐ Will you have DDA discovery records processed by your authority vendor?

☐ If the discovery records are not already compliant with Resource Description and Access (RDA), will you upgrade them to RDA standards?

Deciding to send DDA discovery records to a vendor for authority processing or RDA upgrading depends on another important decision: how long do you plan to keep DDA records in your catalog? If you basically view them as temporary records, perhaps candidates for removal in a year or two, you may not be concerned with their headings being further authorized or meeting RDA standards. If you pay for outsourced work per record sent, you can exclude DDA records from this process and save money. Similar to new acquisition lists, records for outsourced processing are usually extracted based on date cataloged. Nulling out this date in the records will prevent their being tagged for extraction (Downey, 2014). But if the records will be a part of your catalog for the long term, then additional work is in order. This will integrate their access points most fully into your catalog's indexing, bring them up to current cataloging standards, and thereby maximize their discovery. Depending on the source of your records, the cataloging as delivered may already be sufficient.

We take advantage of some free custom edits from YPB, plus we do additional customization using Marc Edit. We have adopted RDA at our institution, however we accept a mixture of RDA and AACR2 e-resource records in our catalog. We plan to send batches of e-resource records for authority processing and RDA upgrades to Marcive at least once or twice a year to take advantage of volume discounts. (We send our other cataloging to Marcive monthly.) Despite our adoption of RDA, we do continue to include general material designators in our title fields (tag 245 subfield h). We believe this is the clearest method to indicate format, particularly for e books. This is especially important in brief title lists of search results in our catalog.

☐ Will you batch upload point-of-purchase records to OCLC to have holdings set?

Whether or not to include DDA records in batch uploads to OCLC will depend on your philosophy and sense of practicality. If you want WorldCat holdings set on all your e-resource records (purchased e-books, e-serials, etc.), then you can include DDA point-of-purchase records too. This may be necessary if you use OCLC WorldShare or WorldCat Local. Maintaining updated holdings in WorldCat is also expected of OCLC member libraries, and needed for participants in OCLC Resource Sharing to borrow and lend e-books, if that is allowed.

Chapter Five

☐ What cataloging statistics do you routinely report?
☐ What statistics regarding DDA discovery records will you need
   to report?

Finally, the question of cataloging statistics comes into play. Whether gathered monthly or less often, most technical services librarians provide statistics on new materials acquired, cataloged, withdrawn, and reclassified. These numbers are typically derived from the catalog. Whether or not to include DDA discovery records in these numbers is an administrative decision, but how to include or exclude them will be the work of the technical services librarian.

☐ How will you handle any local customization of MARC records
   that is required?
☐ How much customization of MARC records will you get for free,
   or pay for, from vendors?
☐ Do you have staff with the time and skill to customize the
   records?

Whether you are batch uploading, outsourcing, extracting, or just plain importing DDA records, you will have to be adept at splitting, merging, extracting, and otherwise monkeying around with files of MARC records. Moreover, if you want to make global changes to some of the fields in all the records, you will need an experienced cataloger who can examine the minutiae of codes and subfields and set up batch edit sequences. One of the best tools for this kind of batch work is MarcEdit, an open source tool for editing MARC records.

In addition to all the file handling discussed in the previous chapter, good old-fashioned cataloging skills will still be required. Before zapping large files to and fro, someone needs to take a close look at the MARC record details and the descriptive bibliographic content. No doubt the DDA discovery records you import will require some local customization. If the vendor offers this for free, it will obviously save money. Even if there is a charge, it will still save time, and therefore money. But if the charge is too high, you can opt to edit the records yourself prior to loading. A vendor may provide some edits to MARC records for free, but charge for others. So you can take advantage of the free editing provided, and then add further local customizations once the records are received. MarcEdit offers many editing capabilities to accomplish this. Paramount among these functions is the creation of "tasks," groups of batch edits to be applied to a file of records all at once. Learning MarcEdit on your own is not too difficult. The best way is to practice editing very small files of records and then scrutinizing them carefully. It is a lot easier to correct errors in your MarcEdit task setup *before* importing them than it is to correct errors in your catalog after they have been replicated. But don't worry, even mass-produced errors can be corrected by re-editing and overlaying records. Granted this dance loses its charm after a while.

☐ Which MARC record customizations or edits are necessary?

☐ What wording will you use to identify DDA discovery records, and what MARC fields will you use for this?

☐ How will you distinguish records from different DDA programs in which you participate, if there are more than one?

Let's address MARC record edits in order of priority. Most critical is that the 856 link to the full text works properly. Naturally the URL has to provide the access that your library's account allows. If your vendor works solely off of IP recognition, then the commercial links may be identical for different libraries, and no customization to the URLs is necessary. If your access depends on a unique base URL (e.g., http://your_institution.vendor_name.com/etc.) then each record's URL has to reflect this.

If off-site access is allowed, then you have two options. A single-sign-on setup with your vendor will automatically refer people from remote locations to your proxy server. No edit to each URL is required. If single-sign-on is not available, then you will need to prepend your proxy server's prefix to each URL in each record. This is easily done by a command in MarcEdit which inserts the prefix in the right place.

The next most important edit to consider is the public note that will display in your catalog as the link to the full text. If you have already adopted a standard for your catalog, such as *Click HERE for full text online,* then you need to add this message to each 856 field, in a subfield z (or 3). If these subfields already exist in the records, but the note given is not what you want, you can replace the message. This is also an easy replace task in MarcEdit, even if the provided messages vary from record to record. You may also want to include text explaining any access restrictions, such as "one simultaneous user" for SUPO e-books.

The next feature that most people will desire is a way to tag all the records for a particular vendor or vendor's collection or sub-collection. There are a number of ways to do this, and your choice of which MARC fields to utilize should take into consideration your local cataloging practices. For example, do the fields display in your public catalog and are they indexed for searching? At our library we chose to tag records by including a corporate author field (710) for the vendor name, and a local series entry (830) labeling it as a DDA record and indicating the source of the MARC record.

For example:

> 710 2   ebrary, Inc.
>
> 830 0   Demand Driven Acquisition (DDA) Discovery Record (YBP)

These tags distinguish each group of records from other e-books in your catalog, both by vendor and type. If your DDA records reflect certain subject areas only, these can also be added to the local tags. And if you participate in multiple DDA programs, perhaps through separate vendors, or with a consortium, you will want to have a different tag for each program.

The question of system control number needs to be answered too. If you desire that all records in your catalog have the same kind of control number (e.g., OCLC number, ISBN, etc.), then to maintain this will require that the number exist somewhere in the delivered records, and that your method of importing the records uses this number as the record's control number. There are advantages to keeping your control numbers consistent, if, for example, you batch upload your records to OCLC to have holdings set. But there are advantages to using a unique system of control numbers for DDA records. Perhaps most importantly, you can be more certain to avoid inadvertent overlaying of other records. The flip side is the possibility of duplicate bibliographic records with different control numbers. Because the inclusion, order, and coding of ISBNs for different formats are inconsistent across records, they are an unreliable match point. Assuming the vendor-supplied records each have a unique control number in their 001 field, the same number can be used in your catalog. See figure 5.1 for an annotated example of a MARC discovery record in MarcEdit View.

☐ Will you enrich discovery records (with tables of contents, for example), or will you only enrich point-of-invoice records?

☐ If the vendor charges for record enrichment, what exactly are they providing and is the enhanced potential for user discovery worth the extra cost?

Finally, if enrichment of records with tables of contents and summaries is available from your vendor, take advantage of that. Even though DDA records may be temporary, and represent only *potential* acquisitions, their *discovery* depends on the completeness and depth of their indexing. Similarly, if the book jackets for their

```
=LDR  01420nam  22003851i 4500        [leader position 5]
=001  ebr10935052                     [vendor-supplied control number with prefix]
=003  NhCcYBP
=005  20140929114853.2
=006  m\\\\lo\\d\l\\\\\\\
=007  cr\|n||||||||||
=008  140929s2014\\\\ne\a\\\\o\\\\\000\0\eng\d
=020  \\$a9048517044 (electronic bk.)   [e-book ISBN correctly coded]
=020  \\$a9789048517046 (electronic bk.)
=020  \\$z9089644466                    [print version ISBN correctly coded]
=020  \\$z9789089644466
=040  \\$aNhCcYBP$cNhCcYBP
=050  \4$aQC7$b.I35 2014                [complete LC call number]
=082  04$a530.1$223
=100  1\$aIcke, Vincent,$eauthor.
=245  10$aGravity does not exist$h[electronic resource] :$ba puzzle for the 21st century
       /$cVincent Icke.               [GMD created despite RDA per local practice]
=264  \1$aAmsterdam :$bAmsterdam University Press,$c[2014]
=300  \\$a1 online resource (109 pages.)
=336  \\$atext$btxt$2rdacontent
=337  \\$acomputer$bc$2rdamedia
=338  \\$aonline resource$bcr$2rdacarrier
=533  \\$aElectronic reproduction.$bPalo Alto, Calif.$nAvailable via World Wide Web.
=588  \\$aDescription based on print version record.
=650  \0$aPhysics.
=650  \0$aPhysicists$xHistory.
=650  \0$aPhysics$xHistory.
=710  2\$aebrary, Inc.                  [e-book vendor name as corporate author]
=776  08$cOriginal$z9089644466$z9789089644466
=830  \0$aDemand Driven Acquisition (DDA) Discovery Record (YBP)
                                        [local series indicating DDA status and vendor]
=856  40$uhttp://site.ebrary.com/lib/dickinson/docDetail.action?docID–10935052$zClick
       HERE for full text online.$xDiscovery records (YBP).
                                        [customized URL provided by vendor]
                                        [no proxy prefix needed for single-sign-on]
                                        [linked text to display in catalog]
=949  \\$aONLINE$wALPHANUM$hE-BOOK
                                        [local holdings, e-book with generic call number]
```

FIGURE 5.1
Annotated MARC Discovery Record (MarcEdit View)

corresponding print version can be displayed in your catalog, as well as author biographies and reviews, the more the merrier. Since these e-books can't be displayed on the new acquisitions bookshelves in your library (or on approval plan shelves), every effort should be made to allow virtual browsing.

Of course, there is no end to the catalog edits that could be made (ask any cataloger), but practicality will limit you to making only those you deem essential or important. Reviewing and improving call numbers and subject headings might ultimately improve access, but the resulting time delay in loading records will negate that benefit. Such higher-level cataloging improvements can certainly be done when titles are purchased, either by overlaying the records with fuller versions, or by editing the point-of-invoice records by hand.

☐ **Do you want your vendor to supply embedded order and invoice data in point-of-invoice records?**

Just as alerts for new discovery records will arrive via e-mail from the vendor, so will notifications of purchases. YBP, as an example, sends weekly alerts via e-mail, showing which titles triggered a short-term loan, and which ones triggered a purchase. They also provide an enhanced point-of-invoice record for each title purchased. The point-of-invoice record contains complete cataloging (although the discovery records are usually quite good already) and acquisitions data in customized MARC fields. This record overlays the matching discovery record and generates an order record to document the purchase in our acquisitions module. We edit the local series phrase from *discovery* record to *point-of-invoice* record, and this allows us to keep a current count of how many records are in each category. Each addition to the purchase group subtracts one title from the discovery group. The point-of-invoice records are now part of the "permanent" collection.

☐ **How often will you remove DDA discovery records that have not been used?**

☐ **What is your plan for removing discovery records for titles pulled from DDA availability by your vendor?**

☐ **What other links may there be to these records, that will need to be addressed prior to removing them from the discovery pool?**

Although you may not have chosen a life span for your discovery records yet, presumably some day you will want to prune the collection of discovery records that have not been used at all. This is similar to weeding print books that have not circulated. You may also want to trim your discovery pool to reduce clutter control spending, especially if your budget cannot support an ever-increasing set of potential acquisitions. If you have a cost associated with the number of records in your catalog, that may also be a consideration leading you to weed out unused DDA records. Perhaps you have included DDA records for titles considered peripheral to your collection policy, since a purchase commitment was not required. You may also decide to wait a reasonable amount of time for book reviews of titles to come out and possibly generate interest. At some point, if the records have still not been used, you may decide that the titles are of no interest. Consider criteria such as length of time without use, publication date, relevance to the library's current collection policy, or other criteria when deciding to remove DDA records from your catalog. If your library already has a weeding policy, consider amending it or adapting it to apply to DDA records. One method is to establish a set time period, perhaps based on typical circulation patterns for your library, after which unused records will be routinely removed from the catalog.

If you decide to remove older discovery records after a certain time period, there are two ways to do this. You could keep a copy of every file you import so you can use them to remove the same records later. This can be done through several steps using, of course, MarcEdit. First of all, use the "MARC join" feature to combine all the older files from which you want to weed records into one file. Then, extract just the DDA e-books that have been *purchased* among the corresponding DDA records in the catalog. This can be accomplished using two flags. (1) the date cataloged should correspond to the date range of the joined MARC file, and (2) when a DDA item is purchased, edit the local series to indicate it is no longer a discovery record, but a purchased DDA item. Then, using these control numbers, remove the corresponding point-of-invoice records from the joined file. Edit the remaining records so the fifth position in the leader is a d (for delete). Load these records back into your system with the function set to delete those records. The same file can be sent to your discovery service, and the extracted OCLC numbers can be batch uploaded to OCLC to remove your holdings.

A simpler way to remove older DDA records is possible if you can extract only the DDA discovery records that were entered in your catalog within a certain time span. If you can do this with confidence that you have not extracted any other records, then you can edit this file to change the leader position 5 to a "d" and overlay the records in your catalog to remove them.

As with any online resource, there is a possibility that outside links will have been made to your discovery records without the awareness of technical services staff. For example, links to e-book records may appear in library guides, online book lists, or course management systems, and these will become dead ends once those discovery records are removed. You should have a plan for how to address this prior to their removal, if only to prepare a response to users who may contact the library with questions.

If your library makes the decision to remove titles from the discovery pool, you should also notify your vendor so that they can update their records. Users can trigger titles directly from the vendor platform, and you will not want to be caught off guard by this.

Finally, some DDA titles will have a surprisingly short lifespan—they will be rendered unavailable by your vendor due to licensing or other issues. Notification of these removals from the discovery pool needs to be responded to promptly. If it is a large number of titles, such as when a publisher stops participating, your vendor will hopefully provide a delete file ready for you to import and do the deed. If there are only several titles at a time to remove, then deleting the records by hand is probably easier than importing files. Either way, you don't want deceased discovery records haunting your catalog and frustrating users with their dead end links.

It is useful for assessment purposes to maintain a record of the titles removed. There may be titles on the list that selectors would choose to firm order. Also, if there is a pattern to the removed records, you can use that information to update your DDA profile.

☐ **In what ways can you streamline the workflow for DDA record processing?**

The cataloging of DDA records should be automated as much as possible. The ideal method would be to program a function in the catalog to respond to alerts of new DDA files, and to retrieve and import those records as soon as they are available. Since this kind of total automation may not be possible, it can be approximated with minimal human intervention. If new DDA records are made available every Monday, for example, then set a task reminder on your calendar to retrieve this file (usually via FTP) every Monday. If it has already been customized by the vendor, then it is ready to be loaded as you would other bibliographic records. If not, then the file must take a short detour through MarcEdit. But as outlined previously, all the edits required can be made instantaneously using a "task," MarcEdit's batch edit function. Then the file is ready to be loaded. Adding new discovery records, and removing obsolete ones, in a timely fashion will improve the quality of your DDA program for your users. In technical services, the workflow should be as smooth as any other function provided behind the scenes for the benefit of the public: reliable and documented, yet open to improvements. See the excellent articles by Lu & Chambers (2013) and Draper (2013) for more on DDA cataloging workflows.

Assessment of DDA

There are a variety of reasons for conducting assessment of your DDA program. The most practical and immediate reason is for a reality check. You want to make sure your DDA program is meeting your goals, and if not, identify possible areas for improvement. Assessment can also inform collection development by identifying specific areas of user interest, and thereby help you appropriately balance your mix of access and ownership. Assessment can also help determine the effectiveness of staffing levels and utilization. Positive assessment results help you communicate your library's effectiveness to others by showing levels of user access and satisfaction, and by demonstrating responsible management of acquisitions funds. Assessment may simply be an institutional expectation or requirement. Finally, assessment provides a source of satisfaction for library staff, demonstrating the fruits of your labor. Common characteristics of successful DDA programs are listed in appendix B, but you should still conduct your own assessment.

Specific questions that DDA program assessment can help answer, and associated data and techniques are discussed in this chapter. Fortunately, with e-books and DDA there is no shortage of available data to examine. In fact, you may find that because e-book data is easy to machine gather, you are drowning in data! Potential sources of data include vendors, the library catalog, order records and financial data, the library discovery layer, user surveys, and feedback from users and library staff.

As you set up your DDA program, try to determine in advance which assessment questions are important for your library. Then determine how you will get the data that will help you address those questions. This will shape how you structure your program so that the necessary data is being gathered.

Librarians typically do not attempt to analyze use of our print collections under such a strong microscope, in part because it would be almost impossible to do so. But this also begs the question, is it always necessary to analyze e-book use to this degree? By no means are we recommending that all of the techniques in this chapter should be used by every library. Use only the ones that speak to your local goals and needs. Ask yourself if the results of a particular assessment will actually be useful to your library, beyond just satisfying curiosity.

☐ What kinds of use and cost data will the vendor automatically provide to help you manage and assess the DDA program?

☐ What other sources of data can readily be obtained from DDA vendors or other systems?

☐ Are there other sources of data that you will need for assessment purposes, and how can you build ways to obtain that data into your DDA program setup?

Your vendors will typically provide reports and data via e-mail alerts and through online administrative systems. Vendors may also be willing to provide custom reports on request, either as part of their overall service or for an additional fee. When starting out with DDA you should familiarize yourself in advance with the data that your vendors will be able to provide so that you know what is practical to obtain, even if you later choose not to actively use all the data points. Ask to see samples of actual reports and a preview of administrative reporting tools before you sign with a vendor.

Ask about the availability of COUNTER book reports. Verify that your vendors will provide all the possible COUNTER book reports that are important to you, and that the vendor is complying with the latest version of COUNTER. There are five book reports in COUNTER Release 4, including number of title and chapter requests, access denied (turnaway) reports by title and platform, and total searches by title. These reports alone are not sufficient for assessing your DDA program, since they do not include any information on expenditures. You will need to know what additional reports are available from your vendor, and you should make sure that individual title-level statistics are available for the various metrics. You will want detailed reports on STL counts and costs, purchase costs, number of superficial uses that don't result in a trigger, and reports that indicate subject by classification system or subject category. Also, if you purchase or subscribe to other e-books from the vendor, confirm that you will be able to get reports that separate out the DDA activity.

If you anticipate that you will want other data for assessment, you should plan your DDA program to collect it. For example, if you want to assess use at a granular subject level, will vendor-supplied reports which assign a classification number to each title suffice? Or will establishing separate funds in your local ordering and accounting system at the start be a more useful way of tracking the data? Choices in how you tag MARC records will also affect your ability to later search for or sort records for assessment purposes. If you have DDA programs going with multiple vendors simultaneously, or participate in both local and consortial DDA programs, planning ahead to enable parsing the data for each program separately will be valuable for assessment purposes.

☐ How will you assess whether your DDA program improves service?

☐ How will you assess user satisfaction with DDA?

☐ How are users discovering the DDA titles (from which access points)? Do you need more access points, or are you promoting the wrong ones?

☐ What other things about your users' behavior does the data from your DDA program tell you, and how can this knowledge be used to improve your services?

Expanded access to a broader array of titles than the library owns is a major reason libraries undertake DDA. Clearly, loading hundreds or even thousands of discovery records in your library catalog provides access to those particular titles. But how are your users making use of these available titles? Does having non-owned titles discoverable alongside library-owned and subscribed collections actually improve service for your local users and result in increased user satisfaction? There are a number of ways you can approach answering these and related questions.

Triggers are the most obvious statistic of interest. It is not unusual for only a small proportion of the discovery pool to actually result in an STL or purchase. However, if no triggers are happening, or if they are very rarely happening it will call into question whether DDA is working for your library. Perhaps the titles are not ones your users actually want, or perhaps your discovery pool is simply too small. Examine more closely the reasons for ongoing low use. The number of unique titles viewed but not triggered may provide an indication of e-books that were not ultimately very interesting to the user. But a use below a trigger threshold can also indicate that only a quick lookup was needed. Some libraries view this "free browse" use as bonus access, albeit superficial, for which the library does not have to pay. The amount of individual books used (number of pages viewed, printed, copied) and the average amount of use per title gives an indication of the extent to which use goes beyond casual browsing.

If usage of specific titles is quite high, you may start to see turnaways. If the use data shows a lot of turnaways, decide if your library should add more STLs or shorten the length of STLs, buy more copies, or upgrade to a multiple-user copy option (if available). If turnaways are only occasional and don't follow any pattern, you may decide to simply accept that some turnaways will occur in any shared collection.

You may also be able to get data that tells you something about the number and type of users benefiting from DDA, such as the number of user sessions. This may or may not indicate truly "unique" users, but is suggestive of whether or not you have a few heavy users, or if use seems to be more distributed across many users. If you require a log-in to use DDA titles, you may be able to get more granular data about users from your own servers. However, privacy considerations should weigh into the decision regarding this level of analysis.

An examination of what is not being used can be as helpful as usage data. Although DDA is a wonderful method for providing access to more titles, more is not always better from the users' point of view. Wading through large numbers of titles to find what you want can be frustrating. By examining the list of titles that are never used, you can gain insight into areas of lesser interest. Look for patterns in the unused titles. Are certain subjects, publishers, or types of material unpopular? Blocking the addition of these records through profiling reduces clutter in your catalog.

User satisfaction can be measured using surveys, either embedded at the point of e-book access, or distributed to your entire population. If you already conduct a general satisfaction survey, you may be able to incorporate a few questions relevant to your DDA program. Users' satisfaction with DDA is intimately tied to their general satisfaction with e-books as a format, including factors such as access, platform software, ability to download, ease of printing, and so on. If your library uses the LibQUAL+ survey, the "Information Control" dimension can provide insight into users' satisfaction with your collections, including e-books. Our institution participates in the Measuring Information Service Outcomes (MISO) Survey every two years. This multi-institutional survey includes standardized questions about use of e-books, satisfaction with library e-book collections, and how important e-books are to users. Similar questions are asked regarding the library's physical collections, allowing us to get a feel for evolving format preferences.

You will also have access to additional "interlibrary loan"-type data if your DDA program includes STLs. Whether or not you are using STLs, you can look for a correlation between implementation of a DDA program and your level of interlibrary loan borrowing. Some libraries have seen interlibrary loan borrowing decrease significantly with the start of DDA, presumably because users have more instant access to what they want, while other libraries have seen no change.

- ☐ Is DDA helping your library meet overall budget goals?
- ☐ Is DDA helping your library make more effective use of acquisitions funding, by directing more spending to materials that are actually used?
- ☐ Is DDA reducing costs for your library?
- ☐ What is the cost of DDA acquisitions in total, and on a cost-per-use basis?
- ☐ How does the cost of DDA compare to traditional acquisitions?

While not all libraries engage in DDA primarily to reduce costs, it is a frequent goal. You can easily assess whether your DDA program is helping your library meet budget goals, and this is useful for demonstrating fiscal responsibility to your institution and stakeholders. Described here are some of the ways libraries are examining the effect of DDA on library expenditures. Which methods you choose will depend on your local goals and priorities.

Your vendor should be able to provide you with the average list price of a title in your DDA discovery pool. This can be used to calculate the value of the entire pool, were you to purchase all the books. This can be compared to your actual expenditures on triggered titles, to determine the potential savings from not purchasing all the books "just in case." Of course, few libraries would even be able to purchase all the books in their DDA discovery pools, but that fact can serve to emphasize the value of DDA. You can also calculate the average cost of only the titles purchased, since this may differ from the average cost of all titles in the pool. This can be compared to the average cost of a print title you purchase, to which you should add physical processing costs, and possibly shelving and storage costs.

If you are allowing STLs, you can calculate the cost of STLs per unique title, as well as your total cost for all STLs. The total cost of all STLs can be compared to what it would have cost to immediately purchase all the titles at full list price on the first triggered use. In this way you can see if STLs are providing additional savings for your library at a program level. If a book is eventually purchased, the cost of prior STLs will be an additional cost which increases the total amount the library spends for an individual title. However, looked at collectively, STLs usually save libraries money, since most titles never trigger multiple uses. If you find that most titles never get past your STL threshold, you may conclude that there is cost savings for most titles, and for your DDA program overall. In its first twelve months, our library's DDA program provided access to ninety-four unique titles that were never used enough to trigger a purchase. By paying only for STLs on these titles, our library saved over $4,000. And it is unlikely that the librarian-selectors or user recommendations could have predicted which titles would get the most use, or would get used at all, out of the many titles published that year. See figure 6.1 for an example of assessment of costs for the first year of DDA at a small academic library.

Since STLs are analogous to an unmediated interlibrary loan transaction, it may also be worthwhile to compare the STL costs to interlibrary loan costs, factoring in staff time as well as delivery costs for a print book vs. the access to an e-book, which requires no shipping.

Average cost-per-use is another metric for assessing the value of a book to the library collection. This can be calculated at the title level, but also at the collection level. You can compare the cost-per-use of e-books acquired through DDA to other e-books your library has acquired via purchase or subscription. Studies at various libraries have found the cost-per-use of e-books acquired through DDA to be the same or lower than the cost-per-use of print books acquired through

7,611	Number of discovery records added to catalog
124	Unique titles triggered
$1,088	Cost for 123 short term loans
$7,588	Cost for 36 triggered purchases
$8,676	Total DDA expenditures (STLs plus purchases)
$14,316	Cost if STLs had not been used
$547,992	Estimated cost if all titles in DDA pool had been purchased "just in case" (average cost per title times number of titles in discovery pool)

FIGURE 6.1
First 12 Months of DDA Costs for a Small Academic Library

traditional approval plan selection. This is primarily due to the much higher use that DDA titles got at those libraries. In other words, even though the initial cost of DDA e-books was higher, the titles were used so heavily that the cost-per-use was reasonable. And because you pay nothing for DDA titles that are never used, on average, DDA programs build collections at a more reasonable cost than traditional acquisitions.

The cost of print and e-book acquisitions, including DDA e-books, can also be compared on the basis of processing costs. Print titles require labeling and security stripping, physical handling from unpacking through shelving and reshelving, and storage space. DDA e-books require additional technical services processing, particularly MARC records management, but do not require any physical handling or storage. Theft, loss, wear and tear, and damage are also not a factor for e-books.

☐ How does DDA help you meet your collections goals?

☐ How does post-purchase use of DDA titles compare to that of other acquisitions?

☐ Do DDA acquisitions represent an ongoing value for the collection?

☐ Is material acquired via DDA "appropriate" for the local library collection? Does it meet your criteria for selection and purchase?

☐ What do the types of titles triggered tell you about the reading activity and research needs of your users?

If DDA is implemented as a strategy for building a permanent collection, one success measure is further use of the titles after the initial purchase trigger. Library studies consistently show that titles acquired through DDA see as much or more ongoing use as traditionally acquired titles. Since ongoing use is a longitudinal research question, check the usage statistics for your purchased DDA titles a few months or a year or more after the initial purchase is triggered. If ongoing use is occurring, than the dollar value of titles purchased via DDA represents ongoing value for the library collection. This use data can also be compared to longitudinal use of print collections, to determine the ongoing value of DDA acquisitions relative to print acquisitions. Libraries have also compared the ongoing use of titles either triggered via DDA, selected by librarians, or purchased following a user's recommendation. This requires a detailed tracking by acquisitions staff, but the data gathered can help inform future acquisitions processes.

DDA can also aid collection development, by helping to identify gaps, or collection areas you did not anticipate. By creating a broad profile for your DDA discovery pool, you can include titles that fit your collection criteria but would not necessarily be chosen for purchase with limited acquisitions funds. For example, you might include titles in your discovery pool that seem a bit peripheral to what is considered "core" for your library collection. If the titles don't get used, no money is wasted, but if they are triggered you now have data on a user interest area that you may not have realized existed. By examining the entire list of triggered titles after a period of time, you may discover patterns of use that suggest subject areas for which you should be acquiring more materials. Analysis of the titles triggered can be compared to your current collection development policy to see if it aligns with the materials your users actually want. Just as you might look at circulation and interlibrary loan data, the data on DDA use by subject, often available by classification number, is a rich source of data providing insight into user behavior. For example, it may identify areas of interdisciplinary research or emerging interest areas of which librarians were unaware. The amount of time a user spends with a single title, and the number of pages viewed, printed, or downloaded gives insight into the depth of use being made.

Alternatively, by examining lists of unused discovery pool titles after the passage of time, you may identify areas in which your users have little current interest. DDA has an advantage over self-reported interests, because it collects data on actual use, not just what people think they might use. Like other libraries, we have found that books recommended by our users do not necessarily ever get checked out, even by the person who recommended the purchase. Of course, there may be valid reasons other than current use for your library to collect materials in lightly used subject areas, but you will be making a more informed decision to do so based on data.

In addition to subject areas, examining other characteristics of DDA-triggered and unused titles can inform collection development. The data may indicate more or less user interest in particular genres or types of literature. Certain publishers may offer more titles of interest to your users. You may also test assumptions about user demand for current vs. older imprints, if both are included in your discovery pool. Other user stereotypes can be tested as well. College and university librarians sometimes assume that science, technology, engineering, and mathematics titles will see more e-book use than social sciences and humanities, but studies at large academic libraries have not borne this out.

If you will want to analyze triggered titles at a more granular level than will be provided in vendor reports, plan how you will automate that parsing. For example, you can categorize DDA purchases by audience level, type of publisher, or genre. Because the number of triggered purchases is often relatively small, some libraries have manually assigned additional categories to the lists provided by the vendor. Of course this is labor-intensive, so each library will need to weigh the time cost against the benefit of this level of assessment.

Librarians are sometimes concerned that unmediated DDA will adversely affect the quality of the collection by leading to "inappropriate" acquisitions. Careful profiling at the start should alleviate this concern, since the librarians control what is allowed in the discovery pool. If you are using a profile based on content characteristics (subject, publisher), then you may decide that your discovery pool has been sufficiently shaped to include only appropriate titles, and that no further assessment is necessary. Of course, even the most carefully thought out approval plan profile can let through anomalous titles. Thus, it can be reassuring to assess the fit of the triggered titles with the library's collection guidelines. Libraries that have assessed appropriateness post-purchase have typically provided the list of DDA-acquired titles to librarian selectors for their review. If unwanted titles are detected, this information can be used to revisit and refine the DDA profile.

You may also wish to examine DDA usage data to identify high-use titles that are candidates for upgrading to MUPO access, or for acquiring additional copies. If you have high-use DDA items on a DRM-restricted platform, you might want to buy versions of those titles on a publisher's platform that has fewer software restrictions.

If you have allowed titles to be duplicated in both print and e-book format, you can compare use data on these to gain some insight into user preferences. Some libraries find that print use of a title declines if the e-book version is made available, but others have found that print circulation of a title remained high when the e-book version was highly used. It is possible that brief e-book perusal leads to increased interest in reading the print version cover-to-cover. Keep in mind the potential effect of differing loan periods when comparing use across formats.

- [ ] In what ways do use patterns suggest you should either restrict or broaden your DDA profile?
- [ ] Are you using the appropriate number of STLs to meet your DDA program goals?
- [ ] How often do titles end up being purchased, after STLs are exhausted?
- [ ] Do manual additions to the DDA discovery pool get used?
- [ ] Should you add retrospective titles to your DDA discovery pool?

☐ Are there patterns to the discovery records that vendors require you to remove? Are there patterns to discovery records that are not being used?

☐ Should you weed the discovery pool, and if so, when?

If for no other reasons, libraries new to DDA should conduct assessment to make sure the program is working as intended. You will not know until after your users are engaging with DDA how effective it is in the context of your local conditions. This can be assessed using much of the same data mentioned above: proportion of items used, unused items, number of "free" uses, triggered STLs and purchases.

If fewer DDA titles are being triggered than you intend, increase the size of your discovery pool. One method is to broaden your DDA profile to include a wider variety of titles. In this way you can include additional publishers, include more subject areas, or even test the interests of your users for titles that librarians consider supplemental or peripheral to your collection. Your interlibrary loan data can suggest areas of high interest to your users that are candidates for DDA. If you are happy with your profile but still want to increase use, the DDA pool can instead be expanded by adding retrospective titles.

If too many DDA titles are being used, narrow your profile parameters to stay within budget, or to avoid purchases out of scope for your library's collection. You should also revisit the price cap on discovery titles, and consider moving it downward. In addition to narrowing your profile going forward, you should also consider weeding the existing discovery pool records in your catalog to reflect the new, tighter focus.

It is possible to add titles to your discovery pool manually, supplementing profiled titles with titles explicitly selected. Assess the value of any such "manual" DDA additions. You can do this by analyzing whether titles added to the pool manually are more likely, less likely, or equally likely to get used as those added through profiling. Some libraries have further analyzed whether titles recommended by librarians or titles recommended by users are more likely to be triggered. One way to track this is to have separate funds assigned depending on how the selection is made. Be sure to weigh the cost-benefit of setting up a simple vs. a complex fund-tracking system. Consider whether or not the level of granular detail provided is likely to affect your decisions and how much extra work it creates for library staff. Compliance is another issue. We found that a complex fund-tracking system was more likely to confuse librarian-selectors. They did not consistently apply funds, rendering the data gathered unreliable. A simpler system provided us with less, but more accurate data that was still useful for assessment and decision making.

Adjusting the number and length of STLs is a common and effective alternative for reducing purchases without reducing the size of the discovery pool. Once you have several months or more of actual use data, you can run the numbers through various hypothetical scenarios to determine the number of STLs that will best help you balance cost and collection building. For example, if you are currently allowing two STLs prior to purchase, what would have been your total costs if you had only allowed one STL? What if you had allowed three STLs? Also look for publishers that go straight to purchase on the first trigger. Some libraries using DDA exclude publishers that won't allow STLs or that have very high-priced STLs, preferring to acquire needed titles from these publishers through selective firm orders or discounted subscription packages.

As mentioned in the cataloging chapter, it is useful for assessment purposes to keep a record of titles removed due to either a vendor requirement or library decision. If patterns can be discerned in the removed titles, profile adjustments can prevent these from being included in your discovery pool in the first place. However, even with careful profiling you will still end up with unused records, and will eventually want to consider weeding your discovery pool. Determining the average time before first use is triggered is extremely helpful in deciding when to weed your discovery pool. You want to have the records available long enough to be discovered, but eventually you will probably want to remove older unused records to prevent your catalog from becoming cluttered.

- ☐ Is DDA worth the staff effort involved? If not, are there ways your DDA workflows could be streamlined, rather than just discontinuing DDA?
- ☐ What is the impact on workload for various units or individual staff?
- ☐ Should staffing allocations be re-thought?

In assessing your DDA e-books program, you should consider all the costs, and compare them to all the potential areas of savings. Costs of a DDA program include the significant staff time involved. Beyond the time required for initial profile setup, there are ongoing staff requirements for catalog maintenance, monitoring, and assessment. There may also be an impact on staff responsible for acquisitions and billing, depending on the extent to which you can roll DDA into your existing workflow. Potential savings in staff time include physical book handling and processing, shelving and reshelving. If you calculate space costs, that is also an area of potential savings. Also, you could compare the cost of a DDA STL to the cost of interlibrary loan for a book, including staff time spent fulfilling the interlibrary loan (at both ends), as well as any interlibrary loan charges and system costs. Your assessment of staff workload should help to determine the sustainability of your DDA program, and may suggest ways in which your library needs to realign staff. It is unlikely that DDA alone will lead to fewer staff being needed, but the type of work required of them will change.

Participating in DDA with a Consortium

Consortial programs are each unique, based on negotiations within the consortium and with the vendors involved. This chapter gives an overview of decisions involved in implementing the most common type of consortial DDA program, involving a shared discovery pool with shared ownership of triggered titles. Examples from the literature on existing consortial DDA projects are used for illustration. Issues discussed in other chapters of this guide will also apply to consortial DDA programs.

Library consortia often have a history of collaboration collection development that makes collaborative DDA for e-books a logical next step. Collective DDA builds on the tradition of sharing through interlibrary loan networks, floating collections, shared print collections, and cooperative negotiation and purchasing of e-resources. A joint DDA program has the potential to save participating libraries the cost of buying titles for which local use and demand may be low. This frees individual libraries to spend funds on materials that are primarily needed locally, or on titles that will see high local use. By building a shared collection of e-books, consortia also have the potential to save money on shipping print books back and forth through interlibrary loan networks.

For individual participating libraries, consortial DDA provides the advantage of collective negotiation of terms with publishers and vendors. Depending on the program design, it may also provide centralized management of many administrative aspects of the DDA program, thus lessening the work required of individual libraries. One of the disadvantages of consortial DDA, is that it can increase the out-of-scope acquisitions for individual library participants. This is a particular problem for multi-type library consortia, where the collection scope of participants varies widely. The potential for duplicate acquisitions is also greater, especially for libraries that have large local collections or that also have individual DDA programs in place.

Consortial DDA should not be relied on to provide titles you expect will be in high demand at your library, such as course reserve titles. It is also not the best approach for obtaining highly specialized titles that only one or a very few libraries will want. As with other shared collections, consortial DDA works best for titles that multiple libraries want to make available, but for which need is not likely to be high at any one library at any given time. It may also be used to address the concern that no library in the consortium will acquire a title as a firm order. DDA can ensure that a needed title is acquired within the consortium, assuming it is used enough to trigger a purchase. For titles in high demand at multiple libraries within the consortium, a shared DDA program can be structured to provide multiple STLs as a supplement to interlibrary loans, or to acquire multiple shared copies.

Though it may seem obvious, it is worth remembering that by its very nature, consortial DDA participation requires relinquishment of local control, and compromises on issues of content, choice of vendors, choice of platform, and other program parameters. Also, it will take several months or more to set up, as there are multiple layers of negotiation involved.

- ☐ Who will coordinate communication, vendor negotiations, setup, administration, and assessment of the DDA program?
- ☐ What role will consortium staff play?
- ☐ How will member libraries be engaged?
- ☐ Is there an existing committee? Will you form a new committee?

The existing consortia structure will influence governance of the program. An existing committee responsible for cooperative collections efforts can be a logical group to steer a DDA program, as they may have already developed a set of relevant, shared goals that can be adapted for a DDA program. However, it may be desirable to form a new committee, to ensure that people with the necessary negotiation and technical skills are on the team. Since cataloging concerns are frequently cited as a challenge for consortial DDA participants, it is highly recommended that an expert cataloger be included on the DDA steering committee from the start.

- [ ] What will the goals for your DDA program be?
- [ ] How will member libraries be engaged during the initial stages of DDA program planning?
- [ ] How will libraries be recruited to participate?
- [ ] What benefits or incentives will entice members to join?
- [ ] Will participation be mandatory for all members of the consortia?
- [ ] What will motivate individual libraries to participate initially, and to maintain their participation?

Many of the same reasons for undertaking a local DDA program apply to consortial DDA. These are described in chapter 1 of this guide, and include expanded user access and cost savings. A shared belief in the synergistic strength of library networks is an additional motivator for undertaking DDA in a consortial setting. Still, given pressures on local budgets and varying institutional priorities, libraries may need to be convinced that the benefits for their users both justify the cost of participating and outweigh the extra workload involved. The Orbis Cascade Alliance mandated participation in their DDA program, but most consortia will need to rely on persuasion to recruit and retain participants (Doyle and Tucker 2011).

Early communication with consortia members will smooth the way for later participation. If the extent of member understanding of DDA is in doubt, consider conducting a survey to educate members about the potential benefits of consortial DDA, to see which benefits are most important to them, and to gauge interest in future participation. Those responsible for administering the program can use the survey results to establish common goals, based on a broad understanding of member needs and motivations. If not already known, it can also be useful to know the following for each member library: library service provider, preferred e-book platform, discovery layer, integrated library system, and whether they also have a local DDA program. It will also be necessary to determine preferred publishers for DDA. This can be done through a survey or through analysis of member acquisitions activity, union catalog holdings, or data for interlibrary loan activity within the consortium.

- [ ] What entity will own the purchased titles?
- [ ] For long-term access of purchased titles, will the consortium host the content? An aggregator? The publisher? What preservation plans are in place?

☐ If there are hosting fees, from what funds will that payment be
made in the future?

☐ Who will sign contracts with the vendor(s), publishers?

In the shared model being discussed here, legal ownership of any purchased
e-books typically resides with the consortium, with member-participants having
ongoing access rights. Most consortia rely on having the content hosted on an
aggregator platform. The same preservation concerns that apply to all e-books will
apply. Formal electronic archiving agreements, such as PORTICO, will help ensure
long-term access to content from participating publishers. The Ontario Council
of University Libraries negotiated rights to load and host DDA-purchased e-books
on their own server to guarantee long-term archival access, but this is unusual
(Davis et al. 2012).

☐ What vendors will you work with? Library service provider?
E-book aggregator?

☐ What publishers will you negotiate with?

☐ What is an acceptable "multiplier" for triggered purchases?
What is the current rate of title duplication within your consortia
for particular publishers?

☐ Will STLs be used prior to purchase?

☐ What will constitute a trigger?

☐ Will other profile parameters apply to titles included in the
discovery pool?

☐ How will the issue of duplication with participant library
collections be addressed?

Consortia typically work with a library service provider and one or more aggregators, usually the ones used by most member libraries. Participating libraries will
have less of a learning curve if they already have existing workflows with the vendors' systems. Libraries which have individual DDA programs will find it easier to
participate in consortial DDA with the same vendors.

The publishers chosen to approach will depend on the preferences of participating libraries. Library service providers and aggregators can assist in the
negotiations that will be required, since they have experience working with many
different publishers. Negotiations with publishers for consortial DDA are reported
to be quite challenging. Publishers are concerned about loss of sales if libraries
pool together and buy a few copies to share. A key point of negotiation in the

most common model for consortial DDA is the "multiplier." For each triggered purchase, an agreed-upon number of single-use copies is purchased at full list price. For example, if the multiplier is five and the title list price is $25, a triggered purchase generates a cost of 5 × $25, or $125. The consortia members then share ownership in five SUPO copies. Unfortunately, some publishers will either not work with consortia for DDA at all, or will demand a higher multiplier than a consortium deems acceptable. Consortia typically propose a multiplier based on a determination of the current rate of duplication of titles among member libraries for a particular publisher. For example, if among the twenty libraries participating in a consortial DDA program, an average of five copies of a publisher's titles are owned, based on past sales, the consortium can reasonably argue for a multiplier of five. If participants have a common library service provider, that vendor can often generate a special report showing existing duplication. Alternatively, holdings in a union catalog can be examined for this analysis.

Decisions and negotiations for STLs and triggers will also be required. Most consortial DDA programs use a greater number of STLs prior to purchase than do individual DDA programs. A NISO survey on consortial DDA found the range was 3 to 25 STLs, with an average of 8 (NISO 2013). As discussed previously, cost considerations and goals related to creating a permanent collection will influence the number of STLs chosen. If possible, more generous triggers should be negotiated for a consortium than for individual library DDA programs, because a purchase trigger results in multiple copies being purchased. Additional parameters will need to be defined for the discovery pool. At the very least a per-title price cap should be stipulated, as well as the publication date of titles to be included in the pool. Additional subject or non-subject parameters can also be specified through profiling, as discussed earlier in this guide.

Duplication can be a significant problem in consortial DDA programs. Any profile must be a compromise reflecting the common needs of all the participants. Large libraries and libraries which also have individual DDA programs are most likely to encounter duplicate purchases and duplicate discovery records. This can reduce the perceived value of consortial participation. One way of minimizing duplicates is to only include new or "frontlist" publications in the consortial DDA pool. If the consortia can create a shared profile, new titles matching it can be added regularly just as they are with individual DDA, and participating libraries can avoid purchasing these, knowing that access will be provided through the consortium. If a shared library service provider is used, they can assist individual libraries with avoiding acquisition of titles already in the consortial DDA pool.

However, individual libraries will have to decide whether they will order those titles anyway, because if the consortial discovery record goes untriggered, the records will likely be removed from the catalog. Duplicates are not necessarily a bad thing. Some libraries holding a title in print will consider access to an e-book version to be an added benefit to users. Unless a library has a MUPO copy, access to additional e-book copies of a popular title can still benefit the users by reducing turnaways. In the end, individual libraries will have to decide whether the amount of duplication that inevitably occurs is acceptable.

- [ ] What can participating libraries expect, and what in turn will be expected of them?
- [ ] Are participants free to advertise or communicate their participation in the program and program details?
- [ ] Will participating libraries continue to have access to any e-books purchased if they later discontinue participation in the DDA program? Will access continue if they ever leave the consortium?

There should be a formal agreement with DDA participants outlining the terms and expectations for both the individual library and the consortium. Participant expectations should specify cost share and who the point of contact will be. Any expectations for both loading and removing records in local library systems should be made clear. Some libraries will need to inform their institution's administration or trustees of their participation. They may also want to advertise participation to their users on websites, or in publicly available reports. If there are to be any restrictions on participants' communications outside the consortium, that should be made clear up-front, along with the reasons why. The agreement should make clear who will negotiate and sign contracts on behalf of participants, what the ownership rights in any purchased e-books will be, and the terms of ongoing access to purchased e-books.

- [ ] How will funding contributions be determined?
- [ ] How will payments for triggers be handled?
- [ ] Who will monitor triggers and expenditures?

The consortium will need to define participants' "fair share" contribution. This can be a particular challenge if there are wide differences in participating library collection size, type, and mission. The size of the user population has most commonly been used to set contribution tiers for consortial DDA. Budget size, collection size, or circulation may also be factored in. Following an initial pilot phase, results of assessment should be used to revisit whether the contribution formula is still considered to be "fair" by participants. If some libraries are shown to be benefiting more than others based on triggered uses, for example, that can be included in a revised formula for future DDA contributions.

Funds are usually collected by the consortium and placed on deposit with the e-book vendor, to be drawn on as uses are triggered. Someone will need to be charged with closely tracking the financial transactions both to make sure there are no billing errors, and also to monitor how quickly funds are being depleted. Due to the large user populations involved, some consortia have found their funds expended quickly, so monitoring should be done daily at first.

- ☐ What access points will participants be expected to make available to their users?
- ☐ If a participating library has other e-books accessible on the same platform, will local e-books be on a separate instance of the platform from the consortial e-books?
- ☐ Will loading of discovery records in local catalogs and discovery layers be required or prohibited?
- ☐ If there is a union catalog for the consortium, who will be responsible for loading discovery records there?
- ☐ Will MARC records be distributed to individual participants, and if so how? Will customization of these records be provided, or will individual libraries have to do that for themselves?
- ☐ What are the expectations for participants regarding loading and removing records?

Loading of consortial DDA discovery records usually requires coordination among participating libraries. Triggers occur more rapidly with a larger user population, so timing the loading of records and removal from all systems is important to give all libraries a chance to trigger uses. Overlapping discovery points may cause problems in assigning costs to the right entity, or in analyzing use data for assessment. If the consortia has a union catalog to which members all contribute records, there is a danger of many duplicate discovery records from the individual library catalogs ending up in the union catalog.

It should be made clear to participants whether discovery records may optionally be, or are required to be, loaded in the local catalog, local discovery layer,

OCLC, local guides and lists, or e-reserves. In the absence of a union catalog, there will need to be a method for distributing MARC records for individual catalog loads. If libraries will be individually responsible for loading records into their catalogs, they will need to add information to both discovery and point-of-purchase records to distinguish the records as part of the consortial DDA program. Methods are described in the cataloging chapter of this guide. Most consortial DDA programs require records to be removed at the end of the program, usually because all funds have been expended. Communications channels will need to be in place to inform catalogers at all participating libraries when to load and when to suppress or remove records. Ideally, advance warning should be given when funds are running low, but before they run out, so participants can be prepared to suppress or remove records.

Additional cataloging and workflows are detailed in an excellent article about consortial DDA cataloging done at the University of Colorado Boulder (CUB). The CUB library serves as a central cataloger for all participants in their consortial DDA program. This gives all participating libraries access to high-quality records, and reduces redundant cataloging efforts within the consortium (Lu & Chambers, 2013)

☐ How will assessment be done, and by whom?
☐ What usage statistics will be possible? Will it be possible to parse usage by participating library?
☐ How will data and reports be made available to participants, and on what schedule?
☐ If an individual library has an account with the same vendor(s) for purchased, subscription, or DDA e-books, will those use statistics be distinguishable from the consortial DDA statistics?
☐ How will feedback from participants be gathered?
☐ What is the plan for final assessment to determine if goals have been met?

The original consortial DDA team may also conduct assessment activities, or a separate person or team may be designated. Many of the metrics discussed in this guide's chapter on assessment will also apply to consortial DDA. In consortial DDA, it will be desirable to assess the benefit of the program to the consortium as a whole, but also to individual libraries. Although participants may appreciate the overall value of the program to the collective, they will also expect to be able to demonstrate a return on their individual monetary and time investment. One of the best ways to show mutual benefit is to demonstrate the extent to which use in general, and triggers in particular, were spread across participating libraries. Vendors may be able to provide use data by Internet Protocol (IP) address range to determine this.

Duplication is a commonly reported concern, and should be part of any consortial DDA evaluation. Libraries can compare lists of DDA titles acquired to their other holdings, to determine what new content has been made available to their users through the program. Return on investment can be calculated by determining the cost of new titles acquired, or titles acquired in a new format, with the amount contributed to participate. Over time, post-purchase usage can be evaluated as a measure of continuing value. Any usage of titles by users at multiple libraries demonstrates the value of a consortial, rather than individual, DDA approach. Cataloging workflow concerns are also a frequent issue, and should also be assessed by surveying participants about the workload impact and any difficulties they experienced. The effect on interlibrary loan within the consortium can also be assessed, since DDA has the potential to improve user service through instant access. Potential cost savings in shipping print books between member libraries, as well as savings in staff time at both lending and borrowing libraries' interlibrary units can also be calculated. The Orbis Cascade Alliance, which developed the first consortial DDA e-book program, has made details of their ongoing evaluation plans and assessment reports available on their website at www.orbiscascade.org/ebooks.

Example of a DDA Workflow Using a Library Services Provider and an E-Book Aggregator

Work with the library service provider to create a profile for selecting titles for the DDA discovery pool, defining subject and non-subject parameters. The library's existing approval plan profile may be used whole or in part for DDA, to streamline work at this stage. For DDA additional non-subject parameters are defined, notably a maximum for the list price for individual discovery pool titles.

1. Enter into a contract with the e-book aggregator specifying the number and length of STLs prior to purchase, and preference for SUPO or MUPO for purchased e-books. Specify the initial deposit or "pledge" amount (minimum total spending promise).
2. The library service provider de-dupes discovery pool candidate titles against the library's existing holdings, and continues to de-dupe against the library's subscription e-book collections and new print acquisitions.
3. DDA-eligible titles are identified in the library service provider's online acquisitions system. Previews of e-books in that system do not result in triggers. Per local policy decision, acquisitions staff do not place a firm order if a DDA discovery record can be made available. Titles not included by the profile may be manually selected for addition to the discovery pool.
4. DDA discovery records are received from the library service provider, locally customized, and loaded in the library catalog weekly. DDA discovery records also appear in the library's discovery layer, providing

an additional access point. Titles are also accessible from the e-book aggregator platform, with no library staff intervention required.

5. When a user triggers an STL, an e-mail alert is sent to designated library staff from the aggregator system. An invoice from the library service provider is generated. Payment is charged to an interlibrary loan "pay-per-view" fund, per local decision.

6. When a user triggers a purchase, an e-mail alert is sent to designated library staff from the aggregator system. An invoice from the library service provider is generated. Payment is charged to the library general "book" fund, per local decision.

7. Point-of-invoice records for purchased titles are downloaded weekly from the library service provider site, and are overlaid on the discovery records in the library catalog. These are full MARC records, including both bibliographic and order information data.

8. A cumulative DDA activity report is received weekly by designated library staff, allowing monitoring of costs and the titles triggered, for both STLs and purchases. More detailed reports are available on-demand from the aggregator's online administrative system.

9. Assessment of the DDA program is conducted annually, and the program is adjusted as needed.

10. Unused records are removed from the DDA discovery pool per the library's retention plan.

Appendix B

Common Characteristics
of Successful DDA Programs

1. Put the work in up-front with vendors to create a detailed DDA discovery pool profile, using both subject and non-subject parameters. An existing approval plan profile may be adapted for this purpose.
2. Place a cap on the list price of titles to be included in the discovery pool.
3. De-dupe the discovery pool against existing print and e-book holdings, including subscribed e-book collections (vendors can help with this).
4. Examine and understand what constitutes a trigger, and select vendors that allow a reasonable period of free browsing.
5. Use 1 to 9 STLs prior to purchase triggering, if cost containment is a high priority.
6. Load discovery records into the library catalog weekly, in addition to providing other access points. Remove discovery records no longer eligible for DDA, per vendor notification.
7. Designate a staff member to monitor expenditures closely throughout the fiscal period, to make sure spending targets are being met. E-mail alerts set up with vendors can help with this.
8. Designate a staff member to monitor use (triggers, turnaways), to address any issues that arise regarding user access. E-mail alerts set up with vendors can help with this.
9. Have a contingency plan, in case spending is over or under that which was anticipated.
10. Assess and adjust the DDA program after the first 6 months to 1 year, and at least annually thereafter.

Glossary

Aggregator. A vendor that supplies titles from multiple publishers on a single e-book platform (e.g., ebrary, EBL, EBSCO, Overdrive, MyiLibrary, JSTOR).

Bibliographic utility. A provider of shared cataloging services and MARC records (e.g., OCLC, Skyriver).

DDA. Demand Driven Acquisition. The acquisition of an e-book by the library at the point in time when the title is actually "used," as defined by the terms of the DDA contract. See "trigger."

Discovery pool. Also referred to as the "decision pool" or "consideration pool." The group of e-book titles made available to library users that have not yet been purchased.

Discovery records. MARC records for titles in the discovery pool, which are included in the library catalog and library discovery layer.

DRM. Digital Rights Management. Various technological means used to "lock down" online content to prevent or limit copying, printing, downloading, or other manipulation of the digital content. DRM may also restrict access to a particular type of e-book reading device. Overly restrictive DRM can be an impediment to convenient and routine uses of e-books.

Library services provider. A vendor that supplies titles from multiple publishers on multiple e-book platforms (e.g., YBP, Ingram/Coutts). Library service providers typically work with aggregators to supply access to e-books. The value-add from using a library service provider as an intermediary comes with acquisitions workflow management, provision of MARC records, and other services.

Manual DDA. Selection of additional, individual titles that are added to a discovery pool that was created automatically using a preestablished profile with a vendor.

MarcEdit. An open source software tool developed by Terry Reese for batch editing and customizing MARC records. http://marcedit.reeset.net/about-marcedit.

Multiplier. Term used primarily in consortial DDA programs that refers to the number of copies of a single title that are purchased by a triggered use. For example, if the multiplier is 3, and the list price of one copy is $30, a trigger will generate a purchase of 3 copies at a cost of $90. Those three copies are then typically shared by all members of the consortial arrangement, subject to the terms of the contract with the vendor.

MUPO. Multiple User Purchase Option. An e-book that can be used by multiple users simultaneously.

Non-linear lending. A purchase model specific to the EBL e-book aggregator (owned by ProQuest). EBL e-books are accessible by multiple users simultaneously, but are restricted to a total of 325 total uses per year, per EBL's negotiated access with the publishers whose titles they make available.

PDA. Patron Driven Acquisition. PDA is often used as a synonym for DDA, however NISO, the National Information Standards Organization, suggests that PDA be reserved for library acquisition of materials based on recommendations by users or analysis of use data. Books acquired in this way may or may not be actually used.

PIPE. Patron-Initiated Purchase of E-books. Occasionally used as a synonym for demand-driven acquisition.

Platform. The e-book interface; the software used to read the e-book.

Point-of-invoice records. MARC records which are overlayed onto discovery records after a DDA title is purchased.

Publisher. A vendor that is the original producer of a title. Most publishers make their e-books available directly on their own company's software platform, which may have few or no DRM restrictions compared to the same title on a third-party e-book platform.

Simultaneous publication. Refers to the publication of a single title in both print and e-book format within a small window of time. Many books are still issued in print first, with the e-book version following many weeks or months later, if at all. Library services provider YBP defines "simultaneous" publication as issuance of print and e-book versions within an eight-week window.

STL. Short-Term Loan. A limited-time use of an e-book allowed by some publishers for some specified percentage of the cost of purchase. The duration of an STL can usually be specified by the library in agreement with the vendor, and common STLs are 1, 3 or 7 days, although longer STLs are sometimes specified. The library may also specify that a certain number of STLs be provided after which an additional use triggers a purchase. The cost of an STL does not typically offset any later purchase of the title, and may be thought of as analogous to an interlibrary loan.

SUPO. Single User Purchase Option. An e-book that can be used by only one user at a time.

Trigger. An action by a user that initiates a short-term loan charge or purchase. Triggers are defined in the vendor contract, and may include user actions such as use beyond any free browse period, viewing of a certain number of pages, printing, copying, and downloading.

Vendor. Used in this guide to refer collectively to whichever commercial service(s) you work with to set up and manage your DDA program. These may include one or more publishers, aggregators, or library services providers.

Works Cited

Baker, Kristine, and Ann-Marie Breaux. 2013. "The Evolution of Academic Book Vendor Services for eBooks." *Against the Grain* 25, no. 2: 20–24.

Carrico, Steven, and Trey Shelton. 2012. "A Real Challenge: Incorporating Patron-Driven Acquisitions Programs into Collection Development Strategies and Budgets." *Proceedings of the Charleston Library Conference.*

Crane, Erin, and Lori Snyder. 2013. "Patron-Driven Acquisition Optimization and Workflows at Liberty University Jerry Falwell Library." *Christian Librarian* 56, no. 2: 75–79.

Davis, Kate, Lei Jin, Colleen Neely, and Harriet Rykse. 2012 "Shared Patron-Driven Acquisition within a Consortium: The OCUL PDA Pilot." *Serials Review* 38, no. 3: 183–87.

De Fino, Melissa, and Mei Ling Lo. 2011. "New Roads for Patron-Driven E-Books: Collection Development and Technical Services Implications of a Patron-Driven Acquisitions Pilot at Rutgers." *Journal of Electronic Resources Librarianship* 23, no. 4: 327–38.

Dinkins, Debbi. 2012. "Individual Title Requests in PDA Collections." *College & Research Libraries News* 73, no. 5: 249–55.Downey, Kay. 2014. "Technical Services Workflow for Book Jobber-Mediated Demand Driven Ebook Acquisitions." *Technical Services Quarterly* 31, no. 1: 1–12.

Downey, Kay, Yin Zhang, Cristobal Urbano, and Tom Klingler. 2014. "KSUL: An Evaluation of Patron-Driven Acquisitions for Ebooks." *Computers in Libraries* no. 1: 10–12, 30–31.

Doyle, Greg, and Cory Tucker. 2011. "Patron Driven Acquisition—Working Collaboratively in a Consortial Environment: An Interview with Greg Doyle." *Collaborative Librarianship* 3, no. 4: 212–16.

Draper, Daniel C. 2013. "Managing Patron-Driven Acquisitions (PDA) Records in a Multiple Model Environment." *Technical Services Quarterly* 30, no. 2: 153–65.

Forzetting, Sarah, and Erin Gallagher. 2012. "A Vendor's Perspective on Consortial PDA." *Against the Grain* 24, no. 6: 30–32.

Forzetting, Sarah, Gabrielle Wiersma, and Leslie Eager. 2012. "Managing E-Book Acquisition: The Coordination of "P" and "E" Publication Dates." *Serials Librarian* 62, no. 1–4: 200–205.

Harwell, Jonathan H. 2012. "ATG Interviews Kristine S. Baker." *Against the Grain* 24, no. 6: 36–40.

Hodge, Valeria, Maribeth Manoff, and Gail Watson. 2013. "Providing Access to E-Books and E-Book Collections: Struggles and Solutions." *Serials Librarian* 64, no. 1–4: 200–205.

Johnson, Robert. 2011. "Purchasing Options in Patron-Driven Acquisitions." *Against the Grain* 23, no. 3: 14–16.

Kaplan, Richard. 2012. *Building and Managing e-Book Collections : A How-to-Do-It Manual for Librarians.* Chicago, IL: Neal-Schuman.

Lu, Wen-ying and Mary Beth Chambers. 2013. "PDA Consortium Style: The CU MyiLibrary Cataloging Experience." *Library Resources & Technical Services* 57, no. 3: 164–178.

NISO DDA Working Group. 2014. "Demand Driven Acquisitions of Monographs: A Recommended Practice of the National Information Standards Organization." NISO.

———. 2013. Demand-Driven Acquisition of Monographs Summary of Survey Results. NISO.

Polanka, Sue. 2012. *No Shelf Required 2 : Use and Management of Electronic Books.* Chicago: American Library Association.

Price, Jason, and John McDonald. 2009. "Beguiled by Bananas: A Retrospective Study of the Usage & Breadth of Patron vs. Librarian Acquired EBook Collections." In *Proceedings of the Charleston Library Conference*, 135–44. West Lafayette, IN: Purdue e-Pubs.

Quint, Barbara. 2014. "Déjà Vu all Over Again: NISO's DDA Report." *Information Today* 31, no. 5: 8.

Roncevic, Mirela. 2013. *E-Book Platforms for Libraries*. Library Technology Reports. Vol. 49, no. 3. Chicago, IL: ALA TechSource.

Shelton, Trey, Tara T. Cataldo, and Amy Buhler. 2013. "EBook Platforms: Lessons Learned from Managing Multiple Providers." *Against the Grain* 25, no. 6: 12–20.

YBP Library Services. 2014. "Annual Book Price Update." YBP Library Services, www.ybp.com/book_price_update.html.

Index